CITY
PLAY

CITY PLAY

BY AMANDA DARGAN AND STEVEN ZEITLIN

PHOTOGRAPHS BY

Martha Cooper, Arthur Leipzig, and other great photographers of urban play

With an afterword by Barbara Kirshenblatt-Gimblett

RUTGERS UNIVERSITY PRESS · NEW BRUNSWICK AND LONDON

**The City Play Project Was Sponsored by
Queens Council on the Arts, Inc.,
City Lore: The New York Center for Urban Folk Culture,
and The Museum of the City of New York**

Library of Congress Cataloging-in-Publication Data

Dargan, Amanda, 1950–
    City play / by Amanda Dargan and Steven Zeitlin ; with an afterword by Barbara
Kirschenblatt-Gimblett ; photographs by Martha Cooper, Arthur Leipzig, and other
great photographers of urban play.
      p.   cm.
    Includes bibliographical references.
    ISBN 0-8135-1577-7
    1. Children—New York (N.Y.) 2. Children—New York (N.Y.)—Pictorial works.
3. Play—New York (N.Y.) 4. Play—New York (N.Y.)—Pictorial works. I. Zeitlin,
Steven J. II. Title.
HT206.D327 1990
305.23′09747′1—dc20
                                                  90-30667
                                                CIP

British Cataloging-in-Publication information available

Frontispiece: Directing Spray, Lower East Side, Manhattan, 1978
(Photo by Martha Cooper)
    Endpapers: photo by Arthur Leipzig. Photo on p. iv, Schomburg Center for Research
in Black Culture, New York Public Library, Astor, Lenox, and Tilden Foundations; on
p. vi, Len Speier, on p. viii, Jack Manning, on p. 209, Marion Bernstein.

Design by John Romer

*For our children, Benjamin and Eliza
and the neighborhood of Sunnyside where
they discovered alleys and sidewalks,
rubber balls, skelly caps, refrigerator boxes,
neighbors, sidewalk cracks, and city children
in the 1980s in New York*

CONTENTS

△ ○ △ ▢ △ ○ △

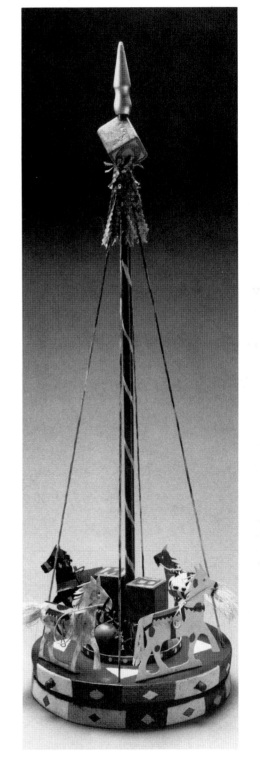

ACKNOWLEDGMENTS

The study and appreciation of play has run up against what Brian Sutton-Smith calls "the triviality barrier," and we want to thank all of those who helped us over it. Robert Baron at the New York State Council on the Arts and Sally Yerkovich at the National Endowment for the Humanities believed in the project early on. Barbara Kirshenblatt-Gimblett, our brilliant and gentle advisor, raised the analytical plane of the project, and cleared the intellectual hurdles. Jean Weiss, former director of Queens Council on the Arts, and Constance Evans, its current director, gave us the freedom to pursue the project. Without these individuals, *City Play* would have never happened.

We also want to thank the staff at the Museum of the City of New York, where "City Play" was on view as an exhibition from May 1988 through February 1989. In particular, we want to thank Associate Director Rick Beard for his insights and comments on the manuscript, and Jane Hirshkowitz, the toy curator, who described herself as the "kiosk," but who in fact was a thoughtful collaborator on the project. Liz Smith, Bonnie Yokelson, and Pam Myers also contributed creatively to the project.

Additional field and historical research for *City Play* was conducted by Margalit Fox, Joseph Sciorra, Sheldon Posen, Nancy Groce, and Susan Slyomovics. We also would like to thank our consultants and informal advisors, Sally Banes, Kate Rinzler, Susan Stewart, Gerald Davis, and Yi-Fu Tuan; in particular, we want to thank Brian Sutton-Smith, Bernard Mergen, and David Nasaw whose work is a testament to play as an activity joyously enacted not on the margins, but at the heart of culture.

We are grateful to the New York Folklore Society, which cosponsored the City Play Project in its early years; our editor at Rutgers University Press, Karen Reeds, who saw the potential in this project for a book; Marilyn Campbell, the managing editor, who shepherded it through copyediting and production; Barbara Kopel, the production manager, and John Romer, the book designer; Mary Scherbatskoy at ARTS, Inc., for sharing her collections with us; Roberta Singer for her common sense and thoughtful reading; and Wendy Wolf (Sargeant Slaughter) for her gentle critique. The City Play Project was sponsored by the Queens Council on the Arts and City Lore with public funding from the New York State Council on the Arts, the National Endowment for the Humanities, and the L. J. Skaggs and Mary C. Skaggs Foundation. *City Play* commemorates the 100th anniversary of the American Folklore Society, which was founded in 1888/1889.

As a husband-and-wife team, we have been inspired by the work of Oscar and Esther Hirschman, who wandered these same New York City streets in the 1930s collecting children's games and compiled a 1,000-page manuscript on the subject under the name Ethel and Oliver Hale, now in the collection at the New York Public Library. Perhaps like the other couples—Iona and Peter Opie, Herbert and Mary Knapp, Ethel and Oliver Hale—who have collected children's games, we have used this as an opportunity to look at our neighborhood, our city, and our culture through a child's eyes, and to see both adults and

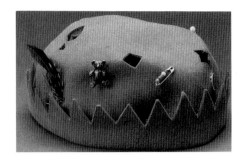

children in all of the endlessly rich manifestations of their playfulness. To all the children whose playful moments we captured on film or tape, and to the adults whose reminiscences we recorded, and the folklorists and historians whose work we drew upon, we, rather than tip our hat, throw it into the air—let's see who can catch it!

A.D. AND S.Z.
NEW YORK CITY
DECEMBER 1989

CITY
PLAY

Arthur Leipzig

PREFACE

"I'll bet you I can jump higher than the Empire State Building."

"Oh yeah?"

"Yeah, the Empire State Building can't jump."

TRADITIONAL CHILDREN'S JOKE [1]

When John Jacob Rascob and his partners transformed the New York skyline by erecting the Empire State Building, they probably never considered that beneath the tower's express elevators the old Sunfish Creek had once formed a natural swimming hole;[2] nor did they imagine that, across the East River in Queens, children would use the lighting of the building in the evening to tell them when to come in from play.[3] Indeed, the architects of American cities did not design stoops for ballgames or rooftops for pigeon flying, and no one considered the hazard to kites when they put up telephone poles. Yet as a result of countless decisions like these, a young person's basic experience of New York gradually changed as streets were paved, as buildings grew upward, as cars pushed children from the streets, as the increasing density led to rooftop games and cellar clubs, and as rowhouses filled once vacant lots.

We begin with the idea that we can understand a place—in this case New York City—by exploring the traditional activities that characterize it. Play can happen on a stoop, a box on the sidewalk, a small part of one block, on one street, in one neighborhood, in one borough, in one city, at one point in history. Yet, it is in this highly localized activity that our experience of the city is shaped. In this book, the words of New Yorkers themselves and photographic images of New Yorkers at play express something of how it feels to grow up in this city, and how that experience has changed over time. Young and old, contemporary and historical, New Yorkers provide the "patchwork of memories, observations, and inferences" that Bernard Mergen suggests must stitch the fabric for a history of children at play.[4]

We began the City Play Project with a public service announcement on television and a story in the *New York Times*. More than a hundred present and former New Yorkers wrote or called to describe their childhood games and memories of playing in the city. These callers ranged in age from twenty to eighty, although most grew up during the twenties, thirties, and forties. Everyone who grew up in the city had some story to tell or memory to relate, so we also conducted many impromptu interviews with cab drivers, waiters, and friends.

In today's New York, we observed and photographed both children and adults at play in urban streets and alleys, in parks and housing project courtyards. We documented teenagers performing feats of daring on their skateboards and bicycles and adults playing bocce in parks and dominoes on the sidewalk. We watched children playing skelly and jumping rope. And over a period of five years, we documented our own children and their friends adapting and transforming an alley in Queens until, as the years progressed, the alley itself became too confined for their stickball games and spilled out onto the adjoining streets.

We watched, too, the unfolding of hip-hop culture, as street play began to intersect with the mass media and the New York arts scene. "In the summer of '78," said a young man named Tee about the early breakdancers, "when you got mad at someone,

Child on a wrought iron fence, Lower East Side, Manhattan, 1978 (Photo ©
Martha Cooper/City Lore)

instead of saying, 'Hey, man, you want to fight?' you'd say, 'Hey,
man, you want to rock?'"[5] We saw breakdancing move from a
form of mock fighting in the streets to the Ritz Ballroom to the
movie screen and back again, until today the youthful Fresh Kid
dancers from New Jersey, who were too young to catch breakdancing in its heyday, self-consciously preserve the tradition.
During these years, New York broke out in "style wars," as
graffiti artists pitted their styles against one another on New
York City trains. From the mid-seventies to the mid-eighties,
Black teenagers set up turntables, speakers, and a mixing board
in parking lots, tapped into the lamppost for electricity, and developed styles of rap singing and scratching (manually maneu-
vering the record on the turntable to create witty, rhythmic
musical effects), until in the late eighties the streets became too
violent to bring expensive equipment outdoors.[6]

PREFACE

Playing Red Rover on the sidewalk, Clauson Avenue, Brooklyn, 1943 (Photo by Arthur Leipzig)

As we watched New Yorkers at play around us, we found many examples of traditional games and improvised play as well as dramatic changes in the play life on New York City streets. Many of the parents whom we interviewed felt that the streets and sidewalks were not as safe for children as they had been in their childhoods (although in truth the streets were never completely safe for children), nor did they feel that the attitude of their neighbors or of city authorities was as tolerant of children's play (although children and adults have fought over the use of public space for centuries).

We also drew on the documentary photography of New York City children and adults at play, most of which focused on low-income neighborhoods. Through their photographs social reformers such as Jacob Riis portrayed the degradation of city life for many immigrant children at the turn of the century. In the 1930s and '40s a later generation of photographers, including Arthur Leipzig and Rebecca Lepkoff, became intrigued by the abundance of children's traditional street games and documented them outside their windows and all over the city. In a special assignment for the *New York Times* in the '40s, Arthur Leipzig set out to find how many games pictured in Breughel's famous painting, *Kinderspielen* (1559) could also be found in New York. Among the eighty games he documented were Johnny on the pony, tip cat, Red Rover, leapfrog, and king of the mountain.

Contemporary photographers such as Martha Cooper captured the inventiveness of New York City's children in their play. In a world where the agendas for children's play often are set by television and the commercial toy industry, one of her goals has been to highlight the creativity of the economically disadvantaged. Before becoming the photographer for the City Play project, Cooper conducted a photographic study of play and discovered that the fashioning of toys from found objects and urban debris still flourished in poorer neighborhoods in the city.

The diaries and reminiscences of nineteenth- and early twentieth-century New Yorkers also provided a rich source of material. *Letters to Phil: Memories of a New York Boyhood, 1848–1856*[7] presents a series of letters written by Edward Eugene Schermerhorn, born in 1842, to his nephew, reminiscing about the more spacious and leisurely New York of his childhood in the 1840s and '50s. A member of one of New York's early and most prosperous families, Schermerhorn talks about flying kites, playing marbles, and lassoing pigs on the unpaved streets.

A number of wealthy New Yorkers who played on New York's streets in the nineteenth century left memoirs detailing the experience. They describe the lives of affluent children in New York, sometimes offering glimpses of working-class lives from their perspective. Nostalgia is such a significant element in the style of the childhood memoir that these works are often more about the process of remembering than about the past they seem to depict. Meta Lilienthal's childhood autobiography, *Dear Remembered World,* about growing up in the 1880s, concludes: "I see New York—not the towering Twentieth Century city—but little, old New York of my childhood days . . . then I realized . . . that the world we remember, the world of our youth, continues to live only within us, and with us will pass into oblivion."[8]

Diaries and reminiscences are often imbued with a kind of nostalgia in some sense antithetical to play. For children, play is not what they did yesterday but today, right now, the second they explode through the door. Play is situated in the moment; it is all present-ness. Play, particularly for children, is action: "We were in perpetual motion, constantly moving."[9] Partly because play is experienced with such intensity it often becomes the most vivid part of childhood. Whatever perspective children have on play comes from anticipation rather than memory. "I was a real child, even though there wasn't much grass. . . . I was

Scratching at a playground party, 142nd Street and Third Avenue, the Bronx, 1984 (Photo by Henry Chalfant)

a true kid—nothing but a kid. I looked forward to every day to go out and play."[10]

Writing about the history of children at play is difficult because in a sense our childhoods are unrecapturable. "A number of thinkers from Freud onwards," writes Brian Sutton-Smith, "have pointed out that our own adult thinking may be purchased at the price of forgetting our childhood years. Our concept of childhood is often a product of our own forgetfulness."[11] Bernard Mergen, who provides a fine sketch of the history of American children in *Play and Playthings: A Reference Guide,* also warns of this danger when he writes, "Butterflies cannot become caterpillars. Much of children's play is a larval stage that leaves a small dry shell into which we try to pack our memories and later experiences."[12] This difficulty of revisiting childhood makes it hard to learn about children's play by interviewing adults or reading their memoirs. The problem is compounded because it is not easy for children to interpret their own play activities, and they leave behind few lasting records of their days at play.

The result is that most people who have written about the history of play have looked at the way adults depict children. In his pioneering work *Centuries of Childhood*, Philippe Ariès shows how the concept of childhood as separate from adulthood is a

Boy in newspaper hat, Harlem, Manhattan, 1947 (Photo by Arthur Leipzig)

relatively recent historical idea;[13] but his evidence is drawn from paintings and other adult documents which show children as "miniature adults." What children were really doing may have differed from the way adults painted and wrote about them, even when they were writing about their own childhoods.

For this book we have drawn on photographic images, oral histories, diaries and reminiscences, observations of and interviews with children, teenagers, and adults, aware of the biases and assumptions of each kind of material. Taken together, these diverse sources offer a view of the city and on play in the city. This is not to suggest that New York, perhaps the most diverse and complex city in the world, is of a piece. What it means to grow up in this city cannot be contained in a set of prototypical experiences of some generic childhood on any composite block, or even in the pages of a single book.

Paul Calhoun

CHAPTER

ONE

Introduction:
Play
in the
Urban
Environment

"There were dozens of games going on at any given time. Whatever was handy would be a base—a dead pigeon, a car, or your little brother could be second base."

DON FELLMAN, BORN 1949,
LONG ISLAND CITY, QUEENS

A neighborhood is at first a confusion of images to the new resident," writes cultural geographer Yi-Fu Tuan. "It is blurred space 'out there.' Learning to know the neighborhood requires the identification of significant localities such as street corners and architectural landmarks, within the neighborhood space."[1] Urban play, particularly outdoor play, is especially revealing in its interactions with the imposed environment. Through play, city objects, often made of metal and concrete, harsh and imposing, are imbued with human values, associations, and memories. Play is one of the ways we develop a sense of neighborhood in a large city. Play is one of the ways a city street becomes "our block."

In New York City, streets, buildings, playgrounds, and schools are often identified by number. But residents speak with great passion about P.S. 155 (Public School 155) or 135th Street. Michael Licht, who grew up on the Lower East Side of Manhattan, recalls an expedition of his gang from Playground #10 to Staten Island, where they burned a giant number 10 into the grass;[2] the first celebrated graffiti artist on New York City's trains was "Taki 183," a youth who lived on 183rd Street in Washington Heights and worked as a messenger traveling by subway, scrawling his name on every available surface. Identified by number, seemingly anonymous places in a crowded city are rendered meaningful through play.

City residents often come to know their blocks almost as the blind come to know their surroundings, in terms of sounds, smells, and textures, "the feel of things"; they discover the uneven bricks along the rowhouse wall, good for a game of points; girls choose to play jacks on the smooth marble stoops to avoid scraping their knuckles on the rough concrete—Marie Stock remembers the "nice sound jacks made on the marble staircases" in Washington Heights.[3] Asked if she could still make a peach-pit ring, which, until recently, city children made by rubbing a peach pit against a wall or stoop until a hole formed in the middle, Martha Verna replied: "After all these years, I know I can find a peach pit. But can I find the right stoop?"[4]

Barging out the door with play on their minds, city children confront stoops, hydrants, telephone poles, lampposts, cars, brick walls, concrete sidewalks, and asphalt streets. Children leaping from the doorway as He-Man and Sheera, or Captain Blood, Superman, or the Knights of the Round Table, have at their disposal an array of swords and shields, which to the uninitiated more closely resemble dented garbage can lids and discarded umbrellas. For the would-be circus performer or ballet dancer, the stoop provides the perfect stage. Those with ball in hand have manhole covers, cars, hydrants, and lampposts to define a playing field. Jumping off ledges, using discarded mattresses and box springs as trampolines, or riding bikes up ramps made from scrap wood, they enjoy the dizzying thrills of vertigo. Each

Girl playing hopscotch, Brooklyn, 1949 (Photo by Arthur Leipzig)

kind of play—vertigo, mimicry, chance, physical skill, and strategy—has its own city settings and variants.[5]

Rural children often have more freedom to roam long distances, away from the watchful eyes of parents. They do not have to share their play spaces with other groups of children or with adults. Coauthor Amanda Dargan, who grew up on a farm in South Carolina in the 1950s, recalls that certain locations where she and her cousins played held special significance but

In the 1980s, Robert Burghardt depicted a wide variety of play activities in two sixteen-foot murals, his visual autobiography of growing up in the German neighborhood of Yorkville in Manhattan, 1926–1938. This is a detail from one of the murals. (Photo © Martha Cooper/City Lore)

that much of the territory in between was not used in play. Children were often on their own and could wander for miles, building playhouses from pine branches and exploring distant forests and fields. If children wanted to play on a hill they had that hill and that was their hill—the stream would be used for something else. City children, more confined, must negotiate the use of space with adults and other children and exploit all the features of their environment; they grow up with vivid memories of every crack and cornice and crevice.

Not all rural children had it so easy. Writing about city children in the period from 1900 to 1920, David Nasaw observed other differences between an urban and a rural childhood: "City kids grew up without adequate air, light, and space to play and grow, but, compared to their rural counterparts locked inside mines, mills, and canneries or put out to work on sugar beet, cotton, and berry fields, they were privileged. The children of the city did not wither and die in the urban air but were able to carve out social space of their own. They converted streets, stoops, sidewalks, alleyways, and the city's wastelands into their playgrounds."[6]

City Play explores in all its dimensions the concept of "turf"— "the defensible territory residents cling to as their own."[7] We focus on three main themes: incorporation, transformation, and control. In the crowded, paved-over city, urban dwellers locate the joy of play by incorporating the features of the urban landscape into their games, by transforming the detritus of urban life into homemade playthings and costumes, and by exerting control over their environment, creating and passionately defending private space.

Many of our examples focus on children because their play, by necessity, is closely tied to their immediate environment. But teenagers and adults also transform their surroundings, and this is a book about play at all ages. We also include many examples of ethnically defined play, but only when it relates significantly to the city's landscape. The ethnic parameters of play, indoor play, the play of wealthier children who play less frequently on the streets, and the relationship of play to immigrant history remain to be studied in more depth.

This photographic essay chronicles the relationship between play and the urban environment. Play began as a dialogue with nature, with children swimming in creeks and rivers, climbing rocks and hills; but in New York City today it is a playful exchange between humans and the world we have constructed for ourselves.

Change over Time

"History is the chronicle of man's concern for place."

MARTIN HEIDEGGER[8]

Pressed and folded by upheavals in the earth's molten core, weathered by the ages, Manhattan schist, a mass of metamorphic rock which runs the length of the island, became the sturdy foundation for New York's tall buildings.[9] Close to the surface in midtown, schist supports the Empire State Building (among a great many other things, the setting for the annual Empire State Run Up, a 1,575-step dash to the top of the building). It dips at about Washington Square and rises again at the south end of the island where the twin towers of the World Trade Center were built.

Similarly, the Triassic Period forged an abundant supply of brownstone in New Jersey, from Paterson and along the Passaic River, and in the Portland region of Connecticut.[10] This red rock was hauled into New York City where it formed the façades of rowhouses known as "brownstones" and became (from the van-

Fast Trotters on Harlem Lane *(now St. Nicholas Avenue), Manhattan, 1870
(Currier & Ives colored lithograph, The J. Clarence Davies Collection, Museum
of the City of New York)*

tage point of children) the backboard for handball and points.
The geological formations in the area around New York led
builders to construct a certain kind of city that shaped the way
city residents played on the block.

Like its hills and rivers and flatlands, changing constantly
with the vast pressures of wind and water, New York City and
its neighborhoods are in a constant state of change, subject to
the pressures of commerce, economics, and immigration; factories manufacture products, goods must be shipped to market,
people need to get to work, and through it all children and adults
find ways and places to play.

"In its early years," writes Michael Winkleman,

> the city was continually growing, expanding, pushing forward,
> gobbling up neighborhoods, suburbs, and small towns in its
> path, urbanizing them, changing the built environment, alter-
> ing the population, and redefining land use. . . . [In Manhat-
> tan] villagers looking for more space developed land just north

of limits of settlement and built new homes. Then, when the city needed more land to house its expanding stores and offices, it too pushed north, right into the only recently established residential neighborhoods—filling in vacant land, displacing residents and changing the neighborhood character." [11]

The marble game was continually overrun.

The population poured along the transportation routes. The opening of the Brooklyn Bridge in 1883 developed areas such as Brooklyn Heights and Park Slope; the opening of the Williamsburg Bridge in 1903 relieved the overcrowding on the Lower East Side, as Jews poured over the bridge into Williamsburg, shifting their stickball games to Brooklyn streets. The subways worked much like the bridges; Coney Island prospered when the trolleys rolled in, and became "the world's playground" when the subways arrived in 1920. The roads in turn worked like the subways; development flowed into the Bronx with the construction of the Grand Concourse in 1909, and children dangerously

Ice skating in Central Park with the Dakota and the Majestic apartments in the background, 1895 (Photo by Byron, Museum of the City of New York)

INTRODUCTION

Looking down Rivington Street from the Allen Street elevated station, Lower East Side, Manhattan, ca. 1940 (Photo by Roy Perry, Museum of the City of New York)

hopped aboard the back bumpers of the Model Ts. As late as 1964, the opening of the Verrazano Narrows Bridge brought a new wave of migration and city games onto the newly developed streets of Staten Island.

Abe Lass, born in 1907, recalls that in June of each year, the city was on the move. All over town, families were relocating, moving to "better" neighborhoods, their old homes often taken by more recent immigrants. Children in his neighborhood waited to see who was moving in, which "new kids" would arrive to undergo the humiliating block initiation ceremonies such as "fire in the church" or "cockalizing." The city's ethnic and immigrant residential patterns were reflected in childhood peer groups, adolescent initiations, and concepts of turf.[12]

In New York, Winkleman argues, "few neighborhoods have been able to persist unchanged for more than ten or fifteen years. A decade may be spent resisting change, and another ten may pass mourning the neighborhood's demise. But then, another definition of the turf surfaces, cast in a new image, with another group to serve."[13]

But while the city's neighborhoods change character with each new wave of residents, its architecture is more stable. By the 1830s, builders and architects began construction that would define New York's play block. In parts of the Lower East Side, "the houses stood in a solid row with no garden space between, although each had its own little backyard. There was likely to be a whole line of identical buildings on one block, erected by the real estate speculators who appeared with the opening up of each new section."[14] Decisions had already been made to conserve space in the city; Manhattan was a narrow island; space was at a premium and even the wealthy were to live in rows of similar houses, not in free-standing homes or estates. By the 1840s, rowhouse construction swept past 14th Street into the Chelsea area near the Hudson River, and children and adults looked to the sidewalks and streets—not to backyards or side yards—for play spaces.

In the mid-nineteenth century kite flying was made illegal in New York below 14th Street. "That restriction," writes George

Steam Boat Wharf, Battery Place, *Manhattan, ca. 1837 (Drawing by Charles Burton, engraving by Stephen Gimber, courtesy of The New-York Historical Society, New York City)*

INTRODUCTION

Rolling tires, Lower East Side, Manhattan, 1977 (Photo © Martha Cooper/ City Lore)

Herland, "may be an important date in the history of childhood in New York, for it may be the first instance on record of child's play having to come to terms with the confined spaces of New York."[15] Yet in 1883 Jacob Riis notes that kite flying continued, "forbidden but not supressed."[16]

The brownstone façade became popular in the 1850s, filling the city with four-story houses with high front stoops, ideal for stoopball and jacks. In 1869, the first apartments were erected on Eighteenth Street, between Third Avenue and Irving Place. These buildings, called "flats," were five stories high and distinguished from the early tenements by amenities such as running water and larger rooms with natural light. The elevator was first introduced in 1850 to haul freight, but in 1870 when the Equitable Building was erected at 120 Broadway, a passenger elevator was installed and the New York skyline began to take its current shape;[17] children learned to adapt their play to this vertical orientation (with "vertical stickball") and to confined spaces (with "box ball").

By the middle of the nineteenth century adults sensed that the pastoral settings for children's play and for adult recreation were vanishing, and plans for Central Park were drawn up in 1853. But when Henry J. Hardenburgh's Dakota apartment house was built at 72nd and Central Park West in 1884, the area was still so undeveloped that it took its name from a humorous expression—it was "so far away it might as well be in the Dakotas!"[18] Early photographs from the Byron Collection depict ice skating and sledding with only the Dakota rising above the trees that border the park. But apartment buildings slowly encircled Central Park, so that by the 1940s, Susan Mildred Brown was able to communicate in code by flashing her bedroom lights to a friend in an apartment across the park;[19] and today, Parnell Jones, born in 1901, finds that the buildings create wind tunnels which send his brightly colored West Indian kites into a tailspin.[20]

With the introduction of gaslight in the 1820s, outdoor sociability and play were extended into the evening hours. In 1880 Brush arc lights were installed on Broadway from 14th to 26th streets, ushering in a new era. In the twentieth century, outdoor lighting made evenings on the block possible on many New York City streets. "It is summer," writes Robert Paul Smith, "and there are the long evenings under the street lamps to talk to girls, to watch the big kids talking to girls, to tease the big kids talking to girls, to be hit by big kids talking to girls, to play Red Rover, to sit on the porch steps and listen to your father tell Mister Fenyvessey what he thinks of the Republicans, to tell your best friend what your father told Mister Fenyvessey and what Mister Fenyvessey told your father, and what words your father used."[21]

With the waves of immigration at the turn of the century, the density of city living defined the experience of city life. Conditions in crowded, poorly ventilated apartments drove New Yorkers out into the streets. As Sylvia Lass said about growing up on the Lower East Side in the 1920s, "My two grandparents, six unmarried aunts and uncles, and I lived in three rooms. The kitchen and the dining room were lined with cots. . . . How could the life not be on the streets, how could it have been otherwise?"[22]

An article in the *New York Tribune* on July 5, 1896, described the overcrowding which resulted from the influx of new immigrants in the late nineteenth century: "When it is called to mind that a certain East Side block has 3,700 dwellers, it is easy to believe that these streets are crowded on summer evenings. And they are, even where the blocks have a much smaller population. Someone has said that there is no standing room at one time on these East Side streets for all the people that live on them."[23]

As the city became more urbanized, the built environment imposed itself progressively on the forms of play, increasingly structuring life spaces. By the 1880s, Gene Schermerhorn was already nostalgic for the open spaces and peacefulness of his 1840s boyhood in New York:

It seems hard to believe that Twenty-third Street—which is the first street in the city of which I remember anything, could have changed so much in so short a time. The rural scenes, the open spaces, have vanished; and the small and quiet residences, many of them built entirely of wood, have given place to huge piles of brick and stone, and to iron and plate-glass fronts of the stores which now line the street.[24]

Schermerhorn was dismayed when the construction for Madison Avenue filled in Beekman's Pond, his old swimming hole. But children adapt to changes in their environment, and the construction sites themselves become play sites. Photographs show children riding on wrecking balls when they are not in use—and Zachary Summers recalls that when construction was in full force on the Belt Parkway, "that was one hell of a great time, those two or three years when they were building an overpass, because when it snowed we would go all the way to the top

Lassoing pigs on Sixth Avenue, Manhattan (Page from Letters to Phil: Memories of a New York Boyhood, 1848–1856, *by Gene Schermerhorn, courtesy of New York Bound Books)*

of the bridge and with a sled we would go all the way down maybe a quarter of a mile."[25]

Each borough developed differently. By the 1840s, Manhattan was already a major commercial center. Brooklyn was developed as a separate but more residential city. As late as 1900, three-quarters of the Bronx was still farmland. Queens was developed still later. Many of its farms were displaced only when the elevated and subway lines were cut through in the 1920s and '30s and as Queens prepared to host the 1939–40 World's Fair. Staten Island remained largely rural until the bridge to Brooklyn was completed in 1964.

Within each borough, neighborhoods and blocks developed at their own pace. In the 1840s, when Gene Schermerhorn was running free "in the wilds above 20th Street," children in Manhattan were being injured in traffic accidents with horse and wagons on Lower Broadway.[26] In the 1920s, while children in Manhattan were racing up and down elevators in their apartment buildings, children in Astoria, Queens, were still snitching tomatoes from local farms.[27] Ultimately, a history of play in New York City must be told block by block.

Gender, Ethnicity, and Social Class

"One difference between being rich and poor is that we rich kids had to outwit all the security that was around us all the time."

SUSAN MILDRED BROWN, 1940S AND '50S,
CENTRAL PARK SOUTH AND WEST, MANHATTAN

How much money a family has, their ethnicity, values, and education, all affect the way their children play. The physical environment—natural and artificial—is one of the parameters of play. Social factors constitute the other.

Each group of children and adults, in each period of the city's history, has had a different orientation to the city's outdoor environment. In recent years, poor children are more likely to be found playing on the street; middle-class children and those from wealthier neighborhoods are more often found in playgrounds, in public and private parks, or attending organized classes. With more generous living spaces, they are more likely to play indoors. Many city parents want their children "off the street," but often only wealthier families can afford alternatives.

Children from low-income families have fewer store-bought toys, and tend to incorporate found objects into their games more frequently than their counterparts who are better off. Wealthier children have the option of leaving the city for summer camp or to country homes; poorer children throughout the city's history have spent their summers confined to the city (unless they are selected for one of the numerous "fresh air" programs to send underprivileged children for a brief stint at camp). Although,

Fifth Avenue near 88th Street in Man-hattan, 1979 (Photo © Martha Cooper/ City Lore)

no doubt, many of these children enjoy their vacations in a rural setting, others whom we interviewed—especially those who grew up in the forties and fifties when the city hosted a more active street life for children—boasted they did not need to go to camp as their street games offered all the companionship and variety they could want. Indeed, some described feeling sorry for the children on the block who were sent out of the city for the summer.

Girls and boys also have different orientations toward space in the city, some of which are enforced by parental controls and social attitudes. Boys are allowed to travel farther from home at younger ages; in many neighborhoods, they dominate the street while the girls congregate on the stoops and play indoors; in our neighborhood they dominate the concrete back alley while the girls are often found on the front lawn.[28] Traditionally, girls have been enlisted to care for younger siblings while their brothers played outdoors.

Historically, fashion and notions of acceptable attire have also limited the play activities of girls; many active games could not be played in skirts and delicate shoes. "Mama didn't like me to play potsy . . . ," writes Sophie Ruskay about growing up at the turn of the century. "Hopping on one foot and pushing the thick piece of tin, I managed to wear out a pair of shoes in a few weeks!"[29] Traditionally, boys' games such as ring-a-leavio and stickball take over much of the street—and games such as "Follow Master" take them beyond the block. Games traditionally played by girls, such as double dutch or hopscotch, are played closer to home. As the dress and attitudes toward girls changed, however, girls' play patterns expanded and, to a more limited degree, their geographical mobility.

Francine Kern, a child growing up in Richmond Hill, Queens, in the '30s and '40s, grew tired of girls' play. Deciding that "playing house was not for me," she

made a proposition to the boys. If I could ride "no hands" for as many feet as they did, they would let me play all their street games. They agreed. When I felt ready all the kids on the block gathered. This distance was marked off and I got up my speed and rode "no hands." When I stopped I knew I had done it. But the resistance to playing with girls was so strong that another test was devised. I was challenged to do it again, but this time with my eyes closed. Well, I did it and when they yelled "O.K.," I was on an unstoppable collision course with a tree. I crashed and rammed my head dead into the tree. I did not cry, did not tell my mother, but picked myself up, straightened out the front wheel of the bike, got on and rode to my yard.[30]

The surfaces of the city become a metaphorical backdrop against which social relations and realities are played out. There are safe zones and danger zones, and zones that belong to the person who is "it." Oftentimes the zones separate girls from boys, or those who are liked from those who are not. In some neighborhoods, gender becomes associated with different parts of the block—or distinctions are made, for instance, between the home and the street, or the stoop and the street. Susan Namm, growing up during the Second World War, remembers the games in her neighborhood: the girls stood on their stoops and waved goodbye; armed with toy weapons, the boys ran down the street to fight the war on vacant lots.[31]

On the block any set of enclosing surfaces can be called a clubhouse and serve as justification for inclusion or exclusion:

At one point the boys in the alley built a clubhouse out of a large cardboard box, and wrote all over the clubhouse, "No girls allowed—especially Alissa." When Alissa saw that she ran home crying. Soon she came back out with a large plate of peanut butter and jelly sandwiches, which she offered to the boys, and by the end of the afternoon they had admitted her to the club. Later I said to her parents, "Alissa had a lot of guts for doing that." But her father said to me, "You know, Alissa hates to have her sandwiches cut in triangles. And when she asked me to help her make the sandwiches, she said, 'Be sure to cut those sandwiches into triangles.' So it was her own kind of poison."[32]

Unlike their rural and suburban counterparts who can find places to play alone and undisturbed, city children like Alissa must find ways to negotiate space and relationships with other children if they choose to play outside.

A major migration of Southern Blacks to the north and three waves of European immigration (the first in the 1840s and '50s, the second from 1880 to 1920, and the most recent beginning in 1964) have made New York perhaps the most most diverse sandlot in the world. Irish and Germans, then Eastern Europeans, Italians, Greeks, most recently West Indians, Asians, and South Americans have had to share the same playgrounds and streets.

The immigrant children who played on the streets between the 1880s and the 1920s connected with an American children's street culture. They played Johnny on the pony, and ring-a-leavio, and potsy (hopscotch). Baseball (stickball when it was confined to city streets) was emblematic of being an American and was a favorite of immigrant children. A traditional story tells of a new immigrant who is handed a tree branch; a friend tosses a ball in his direction, and he ducks. His friend says to him, "Don't do that. Here, hold it this way, swing at the ball. That's how you become an American."[33] Today, there is some evidence that the resurgence of ethnic pride has led new generations of immigrant children to retain more games from their home countries: "Chinese children," says Mary Scherbatskoy, "play Chinese games in a variety of Chinese dialects—Chinese jumprope (using elastic instead of rope), Chinese jacks (using small beanbags), and kick the 'birdie' (made from shredded plastic bags)."[34]

Until the most recent wave of immigration, ethnicity was reflected primarily in the language and prejudices of play: girls jumped in an American style but called it "double dutch" or "double Jewish"; boys played Chinese handball and "baked mickeys" ("micks" were the Irish, and "mickeys," potatoes) in bonfires.

Prejudice insinuated itself into the games of the smallest children. Meta Lilienthal, who grew up in a German family in Tompkins Square and Stuyvesant Park in the 1880s, recalls an episode with one of the first Black girls to move into the neighborhood. Lilienthal tried to introduce Rosie, who was from a small town in Georgia, to her friends in Stuyvesant Park. "'Let me turn the rope for you,' said Rosie, and she picked up the end that I dropped and began to turn."[35] The game continued, until Meta suggested that Rosie should have a turn to jump. Suddenly, the children dispersed, racial epithets were thrown, and

Meta and Rosie stood alone in the park, a "fighting minority."

Different ethnic groups may also have divergent attitudes toward urban space. Abe Lass suggested that Jewish immigrants always had a negative conception of the street.[36] In *Call It Sleep,* Henry Roth describes the envy felt by the Jewish protagonist, David Schearl, of his gentile friend Leo, a latchkey child who is adept at roller skating: "There was no end to Leo's blessings—no father, almost no mother, skates."[37] His sentiments were echoed by Ben Swedowsky, born in 1926, raised Jewish in Spanish Harlem at 110th Street and Madison Avenue:

> We used to fly kites on the roof, and you used that . . . thin wood, from orange crates, put pieces in an *X* and got light-weight paper. [The kite] wasn't just to fly, but an element of war. On the edge of the tail you put razor blades, and you had the advantage if you had the wind, you got your kite over [the other guy's kite], and gave it slack. Then your kite would collapse and cut the line —and the Spanish kids were very skillful at this. I preferred the Spanish kids because they were more adventurous than the Jewish kids who were confined to the house.[38]

In the nineteenth century, too, children of different backgrounds had different orientations toward play in the city. In *The Education of Henry Adams,* Adams recalls a mid-nineteenth-century snowball fight between the Latin School boys from the North End and Irish immigrant children from South Boston:

> A dark mass of figures could be seen below, making ready for the last rush, and rumor said that a swarm of blackguards from the slums, led by a grisly terror called Conky Daniels, with a club and a hideous reputation, was going to put an end to the Beacon Street cowards forever. Henry wanted to run away with the others, but his brother was too big to run away, so they stood still and waited immolation. The dark mass set up a shout, and rushed forward. The Beacon Street boys turned and fled up the steps, except Savage and Marvin and the few champions who would not run. The terrible Conky Daniels swaggered up, stopped a moment with his bodyguard to swear a few oaths at Marvin, and then swept on and chased the flyers, leaving the few boys untouched who stood their ground.[39]

While the Latin School boys stood firm on the steps of their schoolhouse, the Irish children prowled the streets. Adams's recollection, Bernard Mergen suggests, "provides a glimpse of the play of 'slum' children, roaming the streets of Boston until they confront the Latin School boys on their own turf, suggesting that in this period at least, working-class children in Northern cities had considerable freedom in the streets."[40]

The play of "street urchins" has been particularly intriguing to the photographers, journalists, anthropologists, and folk-

Lawn bowlers in Central Park, 1984 (Photo © Martha Cooper/City Lore)

lorists interested in urban play. In today's New York, some youngsters even become accustomed to reporters and tourists taking their pictures. In Washington Square Park in 1986, Guy Trebay was researching a story for the *Village Voice* on trick bikers when he observed a photographer taking pictures of the kids. One of the youngsters, Carnell Jones, lay on the ground with his legs raised in a vee, while a second trick jumper vaulted between his legs and over his head on his bike. Carnell Jones looked up and asked the photographer, "Did you get the pitcher [*sic*]? Are you putting us in the news? Make sure you say that we bought our handlebars with food stamps."[41]

Susan Mildred Brown evokes the play of wealthier children when she talks about the riding camps she attended each summer as a child. "We would be assigned one horse for the summer and fall in love with the horse and then have to tearfully leave it at the end of the summer. And they would give us each a switch from his tail to take home with us."[42] In contrast, John Camonelli talks about growing up during the Depression: "Poor kids didn't have no toys, no money, no bicycles—so we had a 'push-mobile' [a scooter made out of an orange crate and a skate]. We had no horses so we played that we were the horses in Johnny on the pony. When you're poor, the mind creates."[43]

Since this book is about play and the outdoor environment—and poorer children spend more of their play time outdoors—we tend to emphasize the play of poorer children. But we must avoid the seductive stereotype that only poor children are creative; that only poor children play; and that street play is an ideal to which all children should aspire and all parents should want for their children. What begins as a stickball team can end in turf warfare, graffiti, crime, and cannot be seen as separate, idealized, and romanticized. The drug dealers on the Lower East Side keep a running handball game going across the street from the building where drugs are sold. We've heard it said that the tradition of throwing a pair of sneakers over the telephone wires to

Chinese warrior newspaper hat (Collection of ARTS, Inc., Photo © Martha Cooper)

INTRODUCTION

celebrate a local sports victory today signals the location of neighborhood drug dealers. Gang warfare in cities such as Los Angeles has destroyed neighborhoods. In New York City recently, a horde of youngsters went on a rampage of destruction which left one woman near death; they called it "going wilding." Admittedly, isolating play as a subject leads to a certain romanticization of the city; however rich and expressive child's play in the city may be, these positives may not compensate for problems in schools, crime, poverty, and drugs; New York is and probably always has been a tough place to live, and we do not want to suggest otherwise. City play can be violent and dangerous, as well as imaginative.

"Play," writes Barbara Kirshenblatt-Gimblett, "is an arena of choice in many contexts where life options are limited; play can therefore illuminate how children create autonomous and indigenous arrangements in settings they did not build and over which they may have relatively little control."[44] Our goal is to learn from the indigenous adaptations of city children while not falling into a trap of our own devising—a trap that would lead us to conclude that what this city really needs is more vacant lots littered with urban debris.

What Is Play?

Why should you ask for a meaning to play
When it is what I think & do every day,
"To play" is to act what my nature desires
"To work" is to do what my faculties tires.

FROM THE DIARY OF CAROLINE CHESTER,
AGE 14, 1815[45]

"The maturity of man—that means to have reacquired the seriousness that one had as a child at play."

FRIEDRICH NIETZSCHE[46]

Play is a concept that defies definition as it invites efforts to define it. In *Homo Ludens* Johan Huizinga writes, "Play is a voluntary activity . . . executed with fixed limits of time and place, according to rules freely accepted but absolutely binding, having its aim in itself and accompanied by a feeling of tension [and] joy. . . . It stands outside 'ordinary' life as being 'not serious,' but at the same time absorbing the player intensely and utterly."[47] Bernard Mergen writes: "Play is clearly a process rather than a particular activity. Games, on the other hand, involve rules and limits of time and space. Toys are the material artifacts of play and games."[48]

In his essay "Fun in Games," Erving Goffman speaks of play as "focused interaction."[49] It occurs when people effectively agree to sustain for a time a single focus of cognitive and visual attention. Rules of irrelevance tell the players what to ignore.

Man playing yut at the Korean Harvest Festival, Queens, 1984 (Photo by Steven Zeitlin, Queens Council on the Arts)

Rules of transformation tell the players how the real world will be modified inside the encounter. With the outside world held at bay, players create a new world within. A kind of membrane forms around them. They often experience a sense of intimacy, the closeness of sharing a world apart. Ceremonies of initiation and departure are likely to mark the focused gathering.

INTRODUCTION

Certain kinds of action outside the game such as an ambulance going by or a building manager yelling out the window can cause the play scene to "flood out," breaking the spell. When we think of playing fields, we think perhaps of meadows and playgrounds, but a playing field—which can in fact be anywhere—is more akin to a magnetic field that repels forces outside the field of interest and envelops the players with a force as powerful as their concentration.

Mihaly Csiszentmihalyi asked a wide range of Americans why they enjoy activities such as play for which they receive little or no material reward. He concluded that these activities provide a feeling characterized by an unselfconscious sense of absorption, discovery, and exploration. When we achieve the full experience of play, we act within a peculiar dynamic which he characterizes as *flow*. "Action follows upon action according to an internal logic that seems to need no conscious intervention by the actor. He experiences it as a unified flowing from one moment to the next."[50] Players in the city manipulate and adapt the urban environment to achieve that sense of unhindered flow.

Within play worlds, time has its own measures: "We played until it got too dark to see," many New Yorkers told us. Children play until the last reflection of twilight still dimly illuminates a flying ball; they will play until hunger becomes impossible to ignore. "The heat of day, the chill of rain, even the pangs of hunger are not sufficient to intrude on the absorption of a child at play."[51]

In the same way that play fits into the vacant lots and unused spaces in the environment, it is often crammed into the empty lots of time, the space between when the school bus arrives and the bell rings. In the process, it transforms those awkward intervals. Robert Paul Smith writes that as kids, he and his friends "never thought that a day was anything but a whole lot of nothing interrupted occasionally by something."[52] Play is often permitted only when nothing "more important" is taking place in a particular setting or at a particular time. Completely engaged in the acts of throwing, catching, pretending, a child divides time into innings or the time it takes to count to ten for hide and seek, "one Mississippi, two Mississippi." Play time is measured not according to minutes and hours but according to the rules and structures of play; time often goes by in a "split second," metered by the turning of a rope or the rhythm of a rhyme: "Doctor, doctor will I die? / Yes, my child, and so will I. / How many moments will I live? / One, two, three, four."[53]

Play is a child's work; it comprises the largest part of a child's waking hours. As a child grows much of that impulse to play becomes part of work and art and sport and romance; only a small portion of an adult life is any longer thought of as "play." With adulthood, the earlier pleasures of dressing up may lead to a life in the theater; playing stickball on the street may lead to playing baseball as a hobby or a profession; "swiping" potatoes from the local vegetable stand may result in larger thefts, more dangerous crimes; the adult counterparts of these play activities can hardly be thought of as play.

Opposite: Cooking, Lower East Side, Manhattan, 1980 (Photo © Martha Cooper/ City Lore)

At the miniature boat pond, Central Park, 1978 (Photo © Martha Cooper/ City Lore)

To view adult play as nothing more than Scrabble or bingo or bocce or chess does not do it justice; for in addition to our games, there is an element of playfulness which can infuse our work and our art and our personal relationships in much more significant ways. One adult activity, aligned with play and closely tied to the environment, for instance, is gardening; urban horticulture thrives in city settings, reshaping the contours of the landscape, and providing an adult sense of absorption and delight. As Brian Sutton-Smith writes, "To be able to play with children, as well as to be able to play as adults, is perhaps to contain all our ages and all our stages in the same person."[54]

Traditional Games and Improvised Play

"If a jump rope were stretched from New York to California, children all along the way would be jumping to the same half dozen rhymes."

BESS LOMAX HAWES[55]

"A lot of what we did was what you would call improvisational play. I put more value on that, kids just enact an event. It's like unique in all history."

DON FELLMAN, BORN 1949, LONG ISLAND CITY, QUEENS

The scholarly interest in children's folklore in the United States dates from the work of William Wells Newell, who helped to found the American Folklore Society in 1888. Like many of the scholars who documented children's games after him, Newell was primarily interested in traditional games and rhymes which had survived across generations of children. Collecting from both adults and children in Boston, New York, and Philadelphia, Newell believed that the "quaint" rhymes of children were "survivals" and "relics" of ancient song and poetry.

Canal Street, Chinatown, Manhattan, 1983 (Photo by Paul Calhoun, courtesy of the Center for Community Studies, Inc., New York Chinatown History Project)

In his *Games and Songs of American Children,* first published in 1883, he includes a version of Rise, Sally, Rise:

Little Sally Waters
Sitting in the sun,
Crying and weeping
For a young man.
Rise, Sally, rise
Dry your weeping eyes.[56]

Newell's rhyme is accompanied by instructions for a courtship game or "play party" song, enacted by both children and adults in the nineteenth century; at the word *rise* the girl in the center of the ring with her eyes covered stands and salutes the one who pleases her. Newell links the rhyme to a ballad situation united with a dance rhyme in the north of England:

Sally Walker, Sally Walker
　　Come spring-time and love—
She's lamenting, she's lamenting,
　　All for her young man.[57]

　　Many scholars agree that in the early history of games and pastimes in Europe, people of all ages and classes, rural and urban, played largely the same kinds of games. By the eighteenth and nineteenth centuries, upper-class adults had abandoned many of the games they once played, leaving them to their own children as well as to the working class.[58]
　　The version of "Rise, Sally, Rise" that Newell collected includes the refrain:

Fly to the East,
Fly to the West,
Fly to the one you love best.[59]

In the middle of the twentieth century, Leah Yoffie found a version of the same rhyme chanted on the streets of St. Louis. Black girls ended the verse in this way:

Put your hand on your hip,
Let your backbone slip;
Shake it to the east, O baby;
Shake it to the west;
Shake it to the one you love the best.[60]

Similar versions were collected in New York and in Washington, D.C., in the 1970s and '80s, illustrating how a rhyme adapts to a cultural milieu.[61]

Contemporary folklorists believe that children's rhymes are more interesting because of the way they comment on the present rather than the past. Nonetheless, through a century of collecting, scholars have emphasized traditional rhymes and games, transmitted through the generations in fixed phrases: the books of Alice B. Gomme and William Wells Newell in the 1880s and '90s;[62] the work of Norman Douglas in London in the teens;[63] the collections of Herbert Halpert, Benjamin Botkin, and novelist Ralph Ellison with the Federal Writers' Project in the 1930s;[64] the English playground collections of Iona and Peter Opie in the 1960s, which remain the definitive collections in the field;[65] the work of the Knapps in America in the 1970s[66] and Simon Bronner in the 1980s[67] emphasize traditional rhymes, transmitted in fixed phrases, and the rules of traditional games. The rhymes and games gathered in these works echo one another, and their texts exude a fascination with the conservatism of children who pass on rhymes in small variations from one generation to the next. In New York, some of the rhymes have a distinctive urban flavor:

I should worry, I should care,
I should marry a millionnaire.
He should die, I should cry,
I should marry another guy.[68]

I won't go to Macy's any more, more, more.
There's a big fat policeman at the door, door, door.
He'll grab you by the collar and make you pay a dollar.
I won't go to Macy's any more, more, more.

LIONEL SENHOUSE, BORN 1933, BEDFORD-
STUYVESANT, BROOKLYN

Flat to rent, inquire within,
A lady got put out for drinking gin.
If she promises to drink no more
Here's the key to _____ front door.

MAX BRIRENFELD,
OZONE PARK, QUEENS

But though scholars and laypeople have a longstanding interest in traditional rhymes, improvisation has always played a major role in children's play. It was probably as much a part of play in Newell's time as it is in the streets of New York today. He and his successors had other interests which led them to emphasize the games handed down across generations of children.

In fact, Gary Fine writes about "Newell's paradox." On the one hand, Newell suggests that every child "becomes the inventor of legend. Every house, every hill in the neighborhood, is the

locality of an adventure"; on the other hand, he claims that "the formulas of play are as Scripture, of which no jot or tittle is to be repealed."[69] This paradox is at the heart of children's culture. In the 1970s, Bess Lomax Hawes also writes about the "apparently paradoxical co-existence of rules and innovation within play." She observed children playing a game of "monkeys faces" (based on contractor's symbols imprinted in sidewalk cement). The object was to step on all the sidewalk cracks, an exact inversion of another popular neighborhood game, "step on a crack, break your mother's back." She goes on to suggest that "only those cultural items which are susceptible to variation have much chance of survival."[70] Yet, though scholars have noted the improvisatory quality in children's lore, this kind of play has rarely been thoroughly documented or received the attention of traditional games.

Our work emphasizes the improvisatory side of children's lore; children may be jumping to the same rhymes, playing the same games, but they are improvising the materials, developing "house rules," and imaginatively fitting them into city spaces. After all, before a game can be played, the players must agree upon the rules; and in the city, figuring out the rules—deciding just how an abstract set of regulations will apply to this particular space at this moment of time—is as important as the game.

Among the many collectors of children's play, Ethel and Oliver Hale (the pen names for Esther and Oscar Hirschman) were among the few who documented improvised as well as traditional games. While documenting dozens of varieties of games in the 1930s, the Hales would notice something happening on the sidelines such as a young girl standing over a subway grating to feel her skirt blow up puffy and elegant; or a girl with a broken mirror playing with reflections of light or trying to catch the dust hanging in a beam of sunlight; or a group of children imagining that the moon is following them as they walk along their block at sundown.[71]

In our work, New Yorkers often present us with lists of rhymes and games and the rules by which they were played. They want to know if we have heard of ring-a-leavio or tip cat or skelly. But as we observed the children playing in the alley behind our home in Sunnyside, Queens, we were struck by the prevalence of improvised play; unstructured play activities were at least as common as the formal games. We observed the children playing stickball, "line soccer," "duck, duck, goose," hopscotch, jump rope, "red devil," "box," "freeze tag," "cooties," and "hide and seek tag." But we also watched them pretend the concrete overhang above the basement door was a shower, that the set of steps in the backyard was a bus, and that a stone wall was a fortress from which to fight imaginary battles with passing cars. New Yorkers whom we interviewed described improvised activities

Opposite: Playing with light, Lower East Side, Manhattan, 1979 (Photo © Martha Cooper/City Lore)

INTRODUCTION

such as the one described by Isabel Alvarez. She and her sister lived in a basement apartment near "Fort Apache," the police precinct in the Bronx; looking out the small above-ground window, the sisters made a game of counting the feet of the Irish policemen as they marched past.

Traditional games and rhymes are testament to the conservatism of children; but the ways the games are actually played at a given moment of time, the way they are adapted to urban settings, and the way they are improvised reveals the creativity no less important to the legacy.

Arthur Leipzig

CHAPTER

TWO

INCORPORATION

"I was a three-sewer man myself."

BROOLYN RESIDENT WHO COULD HIT A
SPALDEEN THE DISTANCE OF THREE
MANHOLE COVERS[1]

When we played baseball we used a broom handle and a rubber ball. A manhole cover was home plate, a fire hydrant was first base, second base was a lamppost, and Mr. Gitletz, who used to bring a kitchen chair down to watch us play, was third base. One time I slid into Mr. Gitletz. He caught the ball and tagged me out.

George Burns, born 1898,
Lower East Side, Manhattan[7]

ince the first tunnels opened in 1904, New York's subways have profoundly affected not only the city's commercial and residential patterns but also its play life. Beneath the old Third Avenue El in the 1940s girls handclapped rhymes to the peculiar galloping rhythm of the overhead trains;[2] in the '30s hitting a ball over the Third Avenue El marked a home run for children in Yorkville.[3] In Brooklyn in the 1920s, a group of children played a foolhardy game of ring-a-leavio in the subway tunnel between two stations.[4] In Bensonhurst, a group of elderly men adapted an abandoned set of railroad tracks under the El for a bocce court.[5] Inside the trains today, young Black girls take advantage of the roar of the trains to practice their "raps" at the top of their lungs; and, until recently, teenagers tried to go "all city," "bomb all lines" by placing their graffiti insignias on the moving surfaces of cars on every line before the Transit Authority succeeded in squelching the vandals' train art late in the 1980s.[6]

The incorporation of city structures into urban play does not stop with the subways. All over the city, features of the urban

Newspaper boys pitching pennies (Drawing by W.S.L. Jewett, Harper's Weekly, *12 August 1871)*

CITY PLAY

environment are playfully incorporated into the games of children and adults. This chapter explores the ways different features of the city's streets, stoops, brick walls, and lampposts
are built into the play activities—and the memories—of city
residents.

Using the curb, Brooklyn, 1950 (Photo by
Arthur Leipzig)

INCORPORATION

The pulsating city often provides a rhythm for the city's games. Don Fellman, who grew up in Long Island City, Queens, in the 1950s and '60s, still recalls the rhythmic sound of handball as it was played against building walls.[8] He carefully sounds out the syllables: "Puh-TUH-TOOM——buh." This correlated to: palm of hand whacking against ball ("Puh"), ball bouncing off cement ("TUH"), ball hitting wall ("TOOM"), then after a pause as the ball arcs toward the sidewalk, it bounces ("buh"). Often two young girls who don't have a third partner will tie their jump rope to a protrusion on the wall so that one can jump rope while the other turns; or a child will compete against a wall. Catch the ball and score a point; miss and the wall scores. The city becomes a player in the game.

Fishing down a sewer grate, Brooklyn, 1978 (Photo © Martha Cooper/City Lore)

CITY PLAY

The Block

"The boundaries of my youth were defined by one block in the City of New York."

FRED FERRETTI[9]

"144th Street between Brook and Willis Avenues was all America to us."

JIMMY SAVO, BORN 1895, THE BRONX[10]

"Yer out!" 134th Street and St. Nicholas Avenue, Harlem, Manhattan, 1940s (Photo by Nichols, Schomburg Center for Research in Black Culture, New York Public Library, Astor, Lenox and Tilden Foundations)

For many New Yorkers the block is the basic unit of urban geography: it defines community. As Marcia Zeusse put it, in New York, "it was a matter of just one or two blocks that was your land in a neighborhood, and you did not know anything about the people beyond that one or two blocks. New York is little towns—every block is a small town."[11]

The difficulties and dangers of travel in a dense urban center

Hide and seek, Brooklyn, 1943 (Photo by Arthur Leipzig)

are formidable, and New York is characterized by its provincialism; legend has it that there are people who grew up in Brooklyn and never traveled as far as Manhattan. In neighborhoods where gentrification has not driven away small businesses, there are vegetable stands and small groceries on almost every corner: businesses are replicated every two or three blocks, so there is little need to travel far for basic goods and services.

CITY PLAY

"There was a boy named Hod Moore who lived at the Gilsey House on Broadway. . . . One day he took me up on the roof of the Gilsey House and showed me a game he had invented. It was spitting across Broadway. Hod would go right up to the edge of the roof and bend himself way over backwards. Then he would work up a big gob of snot and suddenly he would shoot ahead and blow the spit all the way across the street. Usually it would hit a building on the opposite side before it fell. He would get so excited about it that he would almost fall over the edge of the roof.

Henry Noble MacCracken, born ca. 1882,
Gramercy Park, Manhattan [12]

Jump rope tied to a building, Upper West Side, Manhattan, 1979 (Photo ©
Martha Cooper/City Lore)

INCORPORATION

Playing chicken on the block, Dean Street, Brooklyn, 1943 (Photo by Arthur Leipzig)

The community of children often stages initiations for "the new kid on the block." Born in 1907, Abe Lass remembers how "the whole block gathered around to see who was moving in. The new arrival would then be asked, 'Do you want to play fire in the church?' Of course, the new boy was anxious to please, and said 'yes.' Then we would say, 'O.K. you be the church and we'll be firemen. The new boy was told to yell fire, and when he did all the boys whipped out their little hoses and peed on him."[13] Initiations are compelling evidence of a community of peers on the block, and of the sense of ownership felt by the players for their space.

In contrast to the concept of "the block" is the concept of "the street." While the block connotes an enclosed space, deliminated by street corners, "the street" runs past the corners of the block, connects with the outside world. While "the block" often connotes familiarity, neighbors, relative safety (even though many blocks are unsafe), "the street" is an image of the harsh side of urban life: the cacaphonous sounds of car horns, sirens, and boom boxes; commerce, both illegal and legitimate; strangers and crime. "Street kids" or children who are "streetwise" are those who spend most of their time on the street and who have learned to negotiate its hazards by becoming tough and brazen. Luis Figueroa, a Hispanic man, recalls that as a child he was an "easy mark" in his largely black neighborhood. He was con-

In Flatbush, Brooklyn, a group of boys used to stand on one side of the street and try to pee as far as the other. You know, young boys have elastic bladders and they can really pee a long way. And there would be about twelve boys standing on one side of the street, each one of them creating this high arc going across, and to look at the street, it was really quite surprising.

Abe Lass, born 1907,
Flatbush, Brooklyn [14]

It's all happening on the block, Lower East Side, Manhattan, 1979 (Photo ©
Martha Cooper/City Lore)

INCORPORATION

Gang on the stoop, West 47th Street, Manhattan, 1979 (Photo by Marcia Bricker)

There was a chalk line that went around the pavement all around the block. And it was the understood duty of the children on the block to maintain the line. We all carried sticks of chalk in our pockets, and I remember once that parts of the line were green, and it was a disturbing new element— but it led to other colors. It was in Logan, Philadelphia, between Broad and Olney. It was nice because it was something everybody knew about, you knew that you were doing your bit. It was just "the line."

Joan Roseman,
born 1945,
Philadelphia

tinually hassled by the tougher street kids; then a friend told him to cultivate a "cara palo," a wooden face, tough as nails, unrevealing of an inner self. It worked, but as he grew older he came to realize that he could not pry it off.[15]

"The streets," writes Barbara Kirshenblatt-Gimblett, "were often perceived as a safer place for children to play than parks, if only because the terrain was familiar and there were 'eyes' on the street. Street play was watched, not only from the windows but also as a spectator sport in its own right."[16] A 1913 play survey noted that for every child at play, there were numerous grown-up loungers.[17] Adults observe children at play from the amphitheater of the stoop.

When children play on a residential city block, parents, neighbors, the elderly, as well as older children, can keep an eye on them. The "leash" which holds them is often defined by lines of sight, but it quickly extends to the block. In *Children's Experience of Place*, Roger Hart conducted a study which observed that "in the third and fourth grades, children are allowed to roam as

CITY PLAY

far as 300 yards and those with bicycles somewhat farther. Ten- and eleven-year-olds double their distance, and their free range is often defined in terms of time. They can go anywhere for a certain number of hours."[18] For young children, the block is particularly significant until they are old enough to cross the street and move beyond its boundaries.

As they grow older and suffuse their childhood with meaning, the memories of city residents often become rooted in place. Gaston Bachelard has observed that it is easier to locate memories in place than in time;[19] since places have a physical reality, time

There was always the opportunity to jump the rope or roll the hoople, and several of us achieved the coveted distinction of running entirely around the block … without letting the hoople drop.

Euphemia Mason Olcott,
born 1844,
Greenwich Village[20]

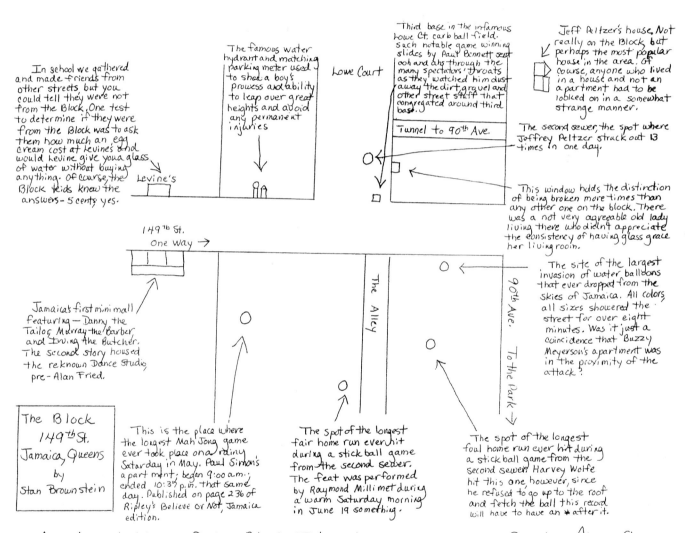

An Aerial View of the Block Taken by Buzzy Meyerson from his Aircraft

Map originally produced for the 149th Street reunion in Queens, May 20, 1988
(From "The Block: An Unauthorized Biography," by Stan Brownstein)

INCORPORATION

is often articulated through spatial metaphors; for many New Yorkers, the block becomes a kind of metaphor for childhood. Memories turn on that patch of turf which they encircled so often on bicycle wheels, and skate wheels, and on foot.

Stoops

"The New York rowhouse," writes Charles Lockwood in *Bricks and Brownstones,* ". . . incorporated several architectural features peculiar to the city. The first-floor parlors rose anywhere from three to twelve feet above the street on a high basement, and therefore, a flight of steps known as a 'stoop' was necessary to reach the front door."[21] The term derives from the Dutch *stoep;* in the Netherlands it was used to raise the main floor of the house in areas subject to flooding. The stoop persisted in Dutch New York, not as a flood measure but, as architectural

---

We lived on a busy street in New Hyde Park, right on the city's border—it was a through street so right in front of our house it was safer to play stoopball than stickball—you were less likely to get run over by traffic. The stoops were mostly two steps high, so you only had two steps to work with. And the stoops were worn thin by people walking on them—so there would be worn stoops and chipped stoops and you got to know those things. These became part of your strategy. If you were going to hit a fly ball you needed to hit a chipped spot; for grounders you needed rounded spots. There used to be Pachysandra shrubbery next to most of the stoops, on my stoop there was a chip on one corner which I could conceal for my opponents' turn, and just casually brush aside when my turn came around. And for your own stoop, you could take a rock and chip a corner. It was never conceived of as an unfair advantage to tailor your stoop.

I was left-handed so I used to throw at the left side of the stoop. And as I think back on this from an adult perspective I realize that there was a left-handed advantage. Doors are designed for right-handed people, and the doors open on the right if you're facing them, so people tend to walk down the right side of the stoop—so the right side is more worn and doesn't give as many fly balls. Most of my friends were bigger and stronger than I was—so my strategies helped to even things out. That was my style anyway. Brains was what I had to work with.

There was a certain feeling to hitting the ball at just the right angle. When you connected like that on the stoop—it's like baseball players when they hit the ball and know it's gone—they don't even have to look. When you hit the stoop at just the right angle, you knew it was gone—over the heads of the fielders into the street—it just had that feeling. I can still remember what that felt like.

Michael Kanarek, born 1948,
New Hyde Park, New York

Opposite: Playing handball on the stoop (Photo by Sara Krulwich, New York Times, *1987)*

Arm wrestling in Harlem, Manhattan, 1941 (Photo by Andreas Feininger, courtesy of The New-York Historical Society, New York)

Down in front of Casey's
Old brown wooden stoop
On a summer's evening
We formed a merry group.

Boys and girls together
We would dance and waltz
While the 'ginny' played the organ
On the sidewalks of New York.

Charles B. Lawlor and
James W. Blake,
"The Sidewalks of
New York," 1894[22]

We played "King of the Hill" on the stoop.

Susan Mildred Brown,
1940s and '50s,
Central Park South and
West, Manhattan

Manhattan stoop, 1930 (Photo by John
Muller, Museum of the City of New York)

Once we got into our heads—the radios at the time were huge things with transformers and radio tubes that were this big inside. So we decided we were going to see if we could unravel the wire in the transformer and go completely around the block with nobody breaking it, so that's what we did—and the kids, one was unravelling it, one was pulling it, anybody that got in the way they say, "See, see, look at the wire." And we almost got around the block, but this service station guy wouldn't allow us around because the cars had to come in and out and he didn't want to be bothered with kids putting a wire around a city block.

Zachary Summers, born 1929,
Brownsville, Brooklyn

INCORPORATION

Girls on stoop, ca. 1900 (Jacob Riis Collection, Museum of the City of New York)

One family went away every summer, and the kids on the block would take over their stoop. Two kids would declare themselves king and queen of the stoop and would decide where each child in the neighborhood was allowed to sit on the stoop. I was allowed to sit only on the cement trim, unless another child didn't show up, and then I was allowed to sit on the bottom step. It didn't help my position any that I had a big mouth and used to yell at people. More than anything I wanted to be accepted by them, but I always felt that I wasn't.

*Robert Rorke, born 1955,
Flatbush, Brooklyn*

historian Andrew Dolkart argues, because it provided a liveable, partially above-ground basement in a city which even in the nineteenth century was becoming pressed for space.[23] Although they did exist elsewhere, "nowhere was the stoop as universal a feature or on so grand a scale as in New York."[24]

By the early nineteenth century, New Yorkers had already developed an affinity for "stoop sitting" on warm summer evenings. In the 1820s, one Englishman raved about the joys of sitting outdoors "on the steps that ornament the entrances of the houses. On these occasions, friends assemble in the most agreeable and unceremonious manner. All sorts of cooling beverages and excellent confectionary are handed round and the greatest good humour and gaiety prevail."[25] Although one architectural critic had accused the stoop of "endangering the neck," for the Englishman, stoop-sitting was so pleasing that it compensated for the burden of climbing the steps.[26]

Lampposts

"To the present generation New York is a city of light. The Gay White Way is known the world over. But the New York that I remember," writes Meta Lilienthal about her childhood in the 1880s,

> knew only gas as the last word in illumination. When the sun set over Tompkins Square, when dusk began to fall, the lamplighter with his long pole came along our block and

The first electric illumination in New York City was tried out on Union Square, and it was there that I first beheld that new miracle, electric light. The bulbs—there must have been a great number of them for the effect was brilliant—were attached to a high pole in the center of the square and the whole thing looked like a beacon light at sea, visible from a great distance. From uptown and down, East Side and West Side, people came to Union Square to look at the great lights. My parents took me there the first evening they were lit and many times afterwards. What fascinated me, even more than the lights themselves, were the strong, dark shadows that they drew upon the walks of Union Square. I had never noticed any shadows there before, but now trees and branches and leaves were outlined as distinctly and sharply as if they had been drawn with charcoal, and the wind swayed these shadows to and fro, which made them more fascinating still. I used to make a game of jumping from one to the other.

Meta Lilienthal, born ca. 1876, Lower East Side, Manhattan[29]

turned on and lit one lamp after another. . . . When night fell every lamp in the metropolis had been lit. And yet my memory of the streets after nightfall was one of darkness, for the lamps, often widely spaced, threw a ring of yellowish light only around their immediate area, leaving wide, dark spaces in between.[27]

Outdoor lighting in the city facilitated evening stoop life and sociability; it opened up the nighttime. The first gaslight in New York dates from the 1820s and, on December 20, 1880, the Brush Electric Company turned on the first electric streetlights on Broadway between 14th and 34th streets, ushering in the era of "Broadway lights."

Over the next several decades city planners believed streetlights might ameliorate social conditions. A 1903 street lighting report called for arc lights on the Lower East and West sides:

It is in these sections that a dense and poorer population lives. This population, in fact, lives on the street, particularly in the warmer months. It is in these sections that the remark can justly be made "that an arc lamp is equal to a policeman."[28]

Hydrants

The first mention of fire hydrants appears in a Philadelphia report of 1801. Ironically, in 1803, only two years later, an assessment report reads: "The hydrants though a very good invention for obtaining a supply of water, either in small or large quantities, have nevertheless been found liable to several objections. The easy access to them by boys and mischievous

Overleaf: East 100th Street, Manhattan, 1970 (Photo by Bruce Davidson, Magnum Photos, Inc.)

We played blind man's bluff on the streets on summer nights under the street lamps—it was a premium kind of spot if you had a street lamp in front of your house because everyone's buddy was down at your house because there was light—so even if you were kind of young you could get into a game once in a while.

Deena Martin, born 1925,
St. Albans, Queens

That's not a fire hydrant, it's a "Johnny Pump." The hydrant is for fighting fires, the Johnny Pump is for fun. . . . That's the Johnny Pump over there— when it's hot like—I'm surprised they didn't turn it on. [Usually] they turn it on full force and leave it on for about half the day. It cools off the whole block. . . . It's like being by the beach, the water cools you off. When it's going, people just sit around the water and it cools off the projects—then they start complaining about four o'clock 'cause when people start coming home from work from the train station they can't get in.

Khadijah Shaheed, born 1958,
Bedford-Stuyvesant, Brooklyn

Directing spray, Lower East Side, Manhattan, 1978 (Photo © Martha Cooper/ City Lore)

persons renders them difficult to be kept in repair."[30] Though the hydrant was to change its form significantly through the years, the mischievous applications of this invention remained as pervasive as its intended use.

Opposite: Children playing on Monroe Street, Manhattan, 1947 (Photo by Rebecca Lepkoff)

CITY PLAY

INCORPORATION

My sister and I used to take empty milk containers, and we'd fill them up with water and dirt. We'd go to the back of the building and we'd fill all the cracks in the building with mud. We were pointing. . . . We had this whole fantasy that the building was staying up just because we were working on it.

Isabel Alvarez, born 1950,
the Bronx

Playing house, Lower East Side, Manhattan, 1966 (Photo by Bruce Davidson, Magnum Photos, Inc.)

CITY PLAY

For generations of New York children, as the sweltering summer draws on, the cry goes around, "Who's got the spanner?" And when some plumber's child or some household with the foresight to have one in readiness or to have made good use of the school metal workshop, opens up the hydrant, the children of the whole neighborhood are drawn to the spot, and, after the joy of the initial wetting devise elaborate rituals of splashing and squirting. . . . By the 1960s the activity was legitimized when the Police Athletic League of New York City, in streets closed off for play, provided sprinkler heads to replace perforated tin cans. But in Mayor Beame's New York of the 1970s the European visitor is still amazed that children can flood whole streets, with the cars swishing through as though there had been a cloudburst.

Colin Ward, A Child in the City [31]

Walls

Many people we interviewed claimed to have grown up on "the best play block in the City of New York." An ideal block always offered a variety of surfaces, and an essential feature was a blank wall, without windows that could be broken in handball games. Ironically, imposing institutions such as warehouses and factories, which look impersonal and uninviting, offer exteriors with significant play potential.

Children playing handball against a wall (Photo by Sheldon Dick, Library of Congress)

A two-story wall at the end of a group of stores that would have no windows—that was a terrific wall. On Merrick Road we had one of those—we played handball for six hours a day.

Mark Podherzer, born 1950,
Flatbush, Brooklyn

We recall a favorite wall of ours, belonging to a brewery, and this had, directly in the playing center, an armorial design of raised bas relief which bore a legend of a sort. This design, which we saw every playing day, we dimly recall to have had a lion's head in the middle of it, but what its meaning was, we neither knew nor cared. But that design was the principal target for our ball, the smooth surfaces surrounding it offered no challenge to our skill; with what deliberate care we aimed at that great, yellow head!

Ethel and Oliver Hale, born 1891,
1893, Harlem, Manhattan [32]

Boy on edifice, Gates Avenue between Clinton Avenue and Vanderbilt, Brooklyn, 1965 (Photo by Builder Levy)

CITY PLAY

"When this cold world starts getting me down," writes New York songwriter Carole King, "and people are much too much for me to face, I climb right up to the top of the stair, and all my troubles rise right into space—up on the roof."[33] The roof, for New Yorkers, has always been both a refuge and a gathering place. Nicknamed "tar beach" by sun bathers, it also fostered such games as kite flying, the dangerous game of rooftop tag, and the sport of pigeon flying. A print from *Frank Leslie's Illustrated Newspaper* in 1878 shows well-dressed New Yorkers escaping the summer heat by climbing up on to the roof in the evening. Photographs by Jacob Riis show turn-of-the-century New Yorkers sleeping on the roof. New Yorkers grow gardens on roofs. In New York, schools and settlement houses construct rooftop playgrounds.

The sport of pigeon flying was introduced to the city by the waves of nineteenth-century European immigrants. Especially popular in Italy, this sport was well adapted to the city where, as Jane Schwartz writes, "clusters of flat-roofed tenements provided the ideal architectural setting for this sky-based sport."[34] Brooklyn neighborhoods such as Williamsburg often provided the ideal social setting; cooperative landlords allowed flyers to build pigeon coops and raise hundreds of pigeons on their rooftops.

The flyers have the New York skyline on their horizon. On a cold, clear morning in Brooklyn, the pigeons fly almost all the way to the Empire State Building. "Far above the cares of the everyday world," write Sheldon Posen and Maxine Miska, "the pigeon-flyer's spirit rises with his birds. The noise and congestion of the streets are far below, while above him his pigeons bank and shimmer in the sky."[35]

Pigeon flyers often call themselves "mumblers" and refer to their birds as "helmets," "tiplets," and "teagers."[36] These are specially bred pigeons and not the garden variety, which flyers derisively call "street rats." The game of pigeon flying pits two of the bird's instincts—flocking and homing—against one another. Opponents wave their flocks into aerial circles which intersect,

---

We had a friend, Michael. . . . He was playing up on the roof. The boys used to jump from roof to roof. That was a big treat for them . . . [and] they used to shoot arrows. They had targets and they'd shoot arrows [from] up on the roof. And he was coming to get an arrow and his shoes were untied, and he slipped and was killed. . . . We didn't see him fall, but we heard him fall, and we went to see him after he was already on the ground. And that was like, so horrible we got afraid of going to the backyard, period. We just stopped going to the backyard. . . . That was really, really bad. He was twelve, I was about ten, and my sister was eight.

Isabel Alvarez, born 1950,
the Bronx

INCORPORATION

We were on the roof a lot, because it was hot. . . . That was my introduction to astronomy—someone had a telescope and it was the first time I saw the stars really and the moon.

Zachary Summers,
born 1929,
Brownsville and
Sheepshead Bay, Brooklyn

Tar beach, midtown Manhattan, 1978 (Photo © Martha Cooper/City Lore)

CITY PLAY

Feeding the pigeons, Third Avenue, Manhattan, ca. 1940 (Photo by Roy Perry, Museum of the City of New York)

and when they do, the birds' dual instincts oppose one another; the birds are pulled toward an enemy flock at the same time as they are drawn toward their owner's rooftop. In a pigeon game, two flocks and hundreds of birds mix in mid-air, and in the melee that follows less trained birds often attach themselves to the enemy flock and are captured by opposing rooftops.

"You chase your pigeons off the coop with a long bamboo pole and then whistle, clap, shout, or wave a flag . . . to keep the birds up in the air and moving toward an enemy stock so they can 'mix' with it. Then, as the stocks split apart, you call your birds home."[37] When a bird is captured, a flyer can either return, keep, or kill the animal depending on his relationship with his opponent. Each move is a point of honor. With these birds, which they feed and nurse with loving care, New Yorkers wage what one flyer calls a war from their rooftop battlements.

People ask me what I get out of pigeons. I could turn around and ask them what they get out of fishing. What they are trying to get out of the water, I am trying to pull out of the sky.
Brooklyn pigeon flyer[38]

INCORPORATION

Rooftop tag . . .

. . . rooftop capture, Lower East Side, Manhattan, 1979 (Photos © Martha Cooper/City Lore)

One winter Fish caught one of Angelo's birds and he tore one of its legs off and sent it back. . . . That little sucker lived another five or six years. Angelo kept him like a pet, he took care of him. He didn't fly with the stock no more, but he was okay. He took care of that bird like he was a baby. . . . Nobody knows why it lived, it was just one of those things. But the next time Angelo caught one of Fish's birds, he took care of him, all right. . . .

Angelo waited till the next day, when he saw that Fish was up on his roof, and he hollered out, "Hey, I'm sending your bird back! Merry Christmas!" And he tossed up the bird, and attached to its leg was one of those little red Christmas tree ornaments, you know those shiny little balls? Only Angelo had filled it with gunpowder, like from a cherry bomb, and lit a fuse to it. That bird was halfway home when it just went boom! Exploded all over the place right in front of Fish's eyes. Everybody in the Southside saw it, that was all they talked about for months. Fish couldn't walk into a pet shop anywhere in Brooklyn that someone wouldn't ask him what he fed his birds that made them blow up in midair. Angelo definitely came out of that on top. The two of them didn't even speak to each other after that. Not a word. They wouldn't even be in the same pet store together. Angelo told me—after Fish was dead—he told me that Fish had come up to him in the street one time and said, "Enough's enough. When are we gonna be friends again?" And you know what Angelo told him? Angelo looks him in the eye, real calm, and says, "Don't worry. I'm just waiting. As soon as my bird's leg grows back, we'll be friends."

Jane Schwartz, from her novel Caught, *1985* [39]

Girls cutting up on the roof, Long Island City, Queens, ca. 1940 (Fiorello La Guardia Memorial Archive)

INCORPORATION

*Pigeon coop outside window, Lower East Side, Manhattan, 1978 (Photo ©
Martha Cooper/City Lore)*

Apartments and Tall Buildings

We used to play vertical stickball.
Rather than have to hit the ball long,
you had to hit it high. If you hit the ball
up to the first floor it was a single, second a double, and so on.

*Phil Hoose, early 1970s,
Chelsea, Manhattan*

Tall buildings changed the lifestyles as well as the skyline of
New York City. Increasingly, New York's visual orientation runs
up and down: "Verticality is essential to the distinctive visual
character of the city," Barbara Kirshenblatt-Gimblett writes,
"summing up as it does the corporate power that determines so
much of city life."[40] Kite flyers in Central Park complain about
wind currents created by tall buildings, and the pigeon flyers in
Brooklyn and the Lower East Side have difficulty flying birds
against one another's rooftops. A recent dispute broke out over a
proposed skyscraper a few blocks from Central Park; New Yorkers fought the construction on the grounds that the building
would cast a giant shadow across the southwest corner of the
park for much of the day.

But tall buildings and apartments harbor their own play pos-

CITY PLAY

sibilities: children communicate with their friends by banging on pipes, they throw matchstick airplanes and water balloons out of windows, sing in the hallways, and trick-or-treat floor to floor in apartment buildings on Halloween. A woman recalls how she and her siblings would open their high window, give a death-curdling scream, and then hide in the closet! In Washington Heights, immigrants from Senegal occupy a building that has been nicknamed the Vertical Senegalese Village, and wealthy New Yorkers in buildings with friendly doormen and frequent visiting tell of the community life that thrives in their vertical settings.

Vacant Lots

"The first thing to understand," writes Robert Paul Smith, "is that the only thing a vacant lot was vacant of was a house."[41] Vacant lots mark a transitional phase in urban development, between the clearing of fields or farmland but before the completion of a rowhouse block. Not exactly forest or field, not exactly house or yard, they have a liminal quality which is part of their appeal. Smith recalls that a particular kind of plant grew there, a plant that burned with a lot of smoke: "It was called 'scribblage.' That is to say, the plant was not called scribblage. The stuff was called that, it was a generic term, something like the word 'junk.' That's it. Junk was manufactured. Scribblage was vegetable junk."[42]

My girlfriend and I used to live in opposing towers in the city (across Central Park). And we used to play *Anne of Green Gables* because there was a part of *Anne of Green Gables* that described the code that they had with switching the light on and off that meant, "Come over immediately, I have something important to reveal." And we knew the code and here were these two towers in Manhattan, and nobody knew that this was these two little girls talking to each other.

Susan Mildred Brown,
1940s and '50s, Central Park
South and West, Manhattan

On our East Side, suffocated with miles of tenements, an open space was a fairy tale gift to children.

Air, space, weeds, elbow room, one sickened for space on the East Side, any kind of marsh or wasteland to testify that the world was still young, and wild and free.

My gang seized upon one of these Delancey Street lots, and turned it, with the power of imagination, into a vast western plain.

We buried pirate treasure there, and built snow forts. We played football and baseball through the long beautiful days. We dug caves, and with Peary explored the North Pole. We camped there at night under the stars, roasting sweet potatoes that were sweeter because stolen.

It was there I vomited over my first tobacco, and first marveled at the profundities of sex. It was there I first came to look at the sky. . . .

Shabby old ground, ripped like a battlefield by workers' picks and shovels, little garbage dump lying forgotten in the midst of tall tenements, O home of all the twisted junk, rusty baby carriages, lumber, bottles, boxes, moldy pants and dead cats of the neighborhood—everyone spat and held the nostrils when passing you. But in my mind you still blaze in a halo of childish romance. No place will ever seem as wonderful again.

We had to defend our playground by force of arms. This made it even more romantic. . . . But the Schiff Parkway was an opponent we could not defeat. It robbed us of our playground at last.

Michael Gold, born 1894, Lower East Side, Manhattan[43]

There will always be some corner of this city the developers can't reach. Some run-down parcel full of garbage that can pass for a backyard. The latest of these fugitive places is a gap-tooth lot with the litter pushed out on Henry Street near Clinton. In that unlikely location, five boys have erected, without easements or grants, Loisaida's first "freestyle" ramp. Made of plywood and two-by-fours, it's an inverted arc or a big half-barrel whose strutted hind end faces a part of Manhattan still left for the poor. The perimeter walls are brick and crumbling, and the ramp fills the space so there's just room enough to fit single-file lines of spectators, junkies as likely as not. A broken piece of signboard hung in this lot says TOYS. . . . Occasionally from within this lot there comes an ominous *phwooont* and a biker goes flying above the lip. Body suspended, he pivots, almost hanging midair, then plummets back onto the ramp in a silhouetted blur.

Guy Trebay, Village Voice, *June 17, 1986*[44]

Trick biker, Lower East Side, Manhattan, 1986 (Photo by Henry Chalfant)

Playing with firecrackers, Lower East Side, Manhattan, 1980 (Photo © Martha Cooper/City Lore)

It was late one summer day when the two men came to my vacant lot. . . . They drove a stake into the ground and nailed up a sign that said, "For Sale." But vacant lots are rough on signs. People bounce balls against them, use them as shields in grass-bomb fights. Dozens of small hands swing from them.

By fall, the sign, dented but still legible, was a tabletop in the clubhouse dug into a hollow—by any logic, more useful than it had ever been before.

Builders seldom leave room for vacant lots. Some of them plan parks, keep the grass neatly cut, the walks neatly trimmed. But they seem fertile, meant for baby carriages, not adventure. Swings don't hang from trees, but from metal frames in neat rows. The land is graded level, and there's no such thing as a touchdown run uphill. . . .

There aren't many vacant lots anymore. The real estate man said they built our house on the last one in our neighborhood. Maybe he thought a vacant lot was a wasted lot. Besides, what kid could raise $15,000 just to keep a lot vacant.

John Barbour, Long Island Press, *1966* [45]

INCORPORATION

Vacant lots often provided the necessary landscape for a widespread New York tradition, "baking a mickey." ("Mickeys" and "Micks" were the derogatory terms for the Irish, and by extension for potatoes, in local slang.) A potato, generally swiped from a vegetable stand, was put in a tin can with a string attached. A bonfire was lit. The potato was cooked, either by swirling the can over the fire on a string, or on a long stick until it "got absolutely pitch black, and then you took it out, you scraped that black off, and the inside was absolutely creamy white. I have never eaten a potato like that anywhere in this country," said Abe Lass, who grew up in Brooklyn in the teens and twenties. "Maybe it's the flavor of my youth that goes with that potato."[46]

The Corner Store

"The candy shops," writes David Nasaw, "were the first and foremost of the small businesses to strike a bargain with the children. . . . [Shops] multiplied in the first years of the century until they were more numerous than even the saloons in the working-class neighborhoods. . . . If the saloon was the workingman's club, the candy shop was the youngster's."[47]

One of the characteristics of the candy stores, remembers Isaac Asimov, was that "they required no education or skill and could be run by a greenhorn as easily as by a sophisticate"—in fact, his new immigrant parents owned one. "As for the owner, he was his own boss, and he could make a living provided he was willing to open the store at 6:00 A.M. and close it at 1:00 A.M." The stores were well suited to the needs of a poor neighborhood, "you could change money, get stamps, buy *one* cigarette."[48]

The corner candy store, situated conveniently on the block, often becomes its cultural nexus. Corners are neighborhood crossroads, natural places for commerce. These stores supply many of the essential toys used by children in the street: rubber balls, jacks, yoyos. In many neighborhoods, its wares become the unofficial currency of children. They buy and exchange trading cards which in the 1940s carried pictures of Indians or flowers, and today depict scenes from movies, such as *He-Man* and *Batman*. They traded the insides of Dixie cups featuring movie stars and ice cream sticks in the 1940s. Later, baseball cards and marbles were bought and wagered. In one neighborhood, a boy collected so many marbles that his friends nicknamed him "Rockefeller";[49] in another, a young man recently drafted into the army called out his window to the children on the block. When they gathered, he poured bags of marbles out the window and watched the youngsters scramble as the glass orbs bounced and clattered wildly on the sidewalk.

Opposite: Boy "dying" in vacant lot, Dean Street, Brooklyn, ca. 1943 (Photo by Arthur Leipzig)

The candy store was a hangout, and the big thing was to get a Mickey Mantle card, everybody wanted it. I have a Mickey Mantle card. And there's a '56 and a '57 Mantle, and they would trade you fifty or one hundred cards to get it.

And every three to six months there were different games—first it was spring, and yoyos would come in, and the candy store would sell yoyos, and to promote them there would be a man from Duncan Yoyos who would come to the local theater and he would run a contest with a prize if you could imitate him doing things like "rock the baby." Next would be tops, in the summer, or ball. The candy stores would sell whatever was popular to play.

Benjamin Chiaro, Jr., born 1947, Hoboken, New Jersey

Lucky Good Humor ice cream sticks were our currency. You could get the aggie of your choice for, say, five sticks, or the use of a bike for an hour for four sticks. This was distinctly different from bargaining or bartering. . . . You could ask for something back if you traded. But if ice cream sticks had changed hands—no returns or refunds.

Francine Kern, born 1932, Richmond Hill, Queens

The Spaldeen was a staple at the corner store (Photo © Martha Cooper/City Lore)

The corner store—that was where all the great thinkers congregated. There was Jay Rosen, Happy Jack and Big Bob, and Sad Sack. These were the guys who would sip and drink their sodas, you could get nickel sodas and dime ice creams, and they had syrups—lemon, cherry, and chocolate, the three essential flavors.

The store had a pinball machine, and many were the times if you didn't have money for the game you could go and watch the older guys—who had paper routes—play the machine.

And you would listen and watch and try to get the body language with the machine, figure out which way you could shake the machine and increase your score. There were numbers hand-drawn on the machine to help you figure out which was the best way to draw back on the lever to get the ball in just the right lane.

So I would stand and watch, at the age of ten, with my head just above the machine. And [twenty years later] when I was a student in medical school watching surgery and I knew I couldn't ask a question or make a sound, I would be reminded of those days—they had the same quietude and awe.

Richard Wallace, born 1949, Philadelphia

Today, bodegas (groceries) have replaced the corner store in many Hispanic neighborhoods; in others, the function has been taken over by the new video rental stores, which often feature video games and sell candy as well. Despite changes, the corner crossroads remain part of growing up in the city.

Surfaces

For a nineteenth-century child growing up in a largely unpaved city, the earth was basically dirt, "clean dirt," Gene Schermerhorn called it, "nature's gift to boyhood."[50] But when the paving of New York's streets began in the late nineteenth century, Jacob Riis, journalist, photographer, and social reformer, reinterpreted the once ubiquitous red earth. It was no longer simply earth, and it was no longer "clean." It was what anthropologist Mary Douglas has termed "matter out of place."[51] Earth became dirt—with all its connotations of filth.

On the unpaved streets of the Lower East Side, the dirt on the bare feet and hands of poor immigrant children became a symbol of their deprivation. The writings of Jacob Riis are populated with mud-smudged children hurling dirt balls. He associates dirt with poor hygiene, and with bathtubs in the kitchen. "In the tenements," he writes, "children and the dirt are sworn and loyal friends. In his early raids upon the established order of society, the gutter backs the boy up to the best of its ability. [Whether] it is a mission to be raided, or a 'dutch' grocer's shop, or a parade of the rival gang from the next block, the gutter furnishes ammunition that is always handy."[52] When Riis writes

about a group of boys who stole an American flag from the door of a church, he attributes the cause of their delinquency to "the dirt . . . in other words: the slum."[53]

Yet as Riis was writing this passage in *Children of the Poor,* he observed that "a transformation was being worked in some of the filthiest streets on the East Side by a combination of new asphalt pavements with a greatly improved cleaning service."[54] Deficiencies in the "three Rs," Riis believed, might be corrected if attention were paid to the "three Ds—Dirt, Discomfort, and Disease."[55]

Spinning tops, Brooklyn, 1943 (Photo by Arthur Leipzig)

We always carried a spaldeen in our pockets. When we rode our bikes, we carried it in the spokes of the wheel.
David Chapman, born 1950s, Brooklyn

I lived on roller skates. . . . Sidewalks were identified by their texture—some corrugated or scored with wavy grooves that could trip you, some of rough concrete that buzzed the soles of your feet, others of smooth slate that allowed maximum speed. . . .

I knew the feel of each bit of sidewalk so well that I could have skated to the corner of Fifth Avenue and, without raising my eyes, told which house I was passing, and then gone on to describe its inhabitants and the friendliness or reverse of the furnaceman, the butler and the cook.

Hamilton Fish Armstrong, born 1893, Greenwich Village, Manhattan[56]

Robert Day roller skating on 126th Street, Harlem, Manhattan, 1939 (Photo by Morgan and Marvin Smith, Schomburg Center for Research in Black Culture, New York Public Library, Astor, Lenox, and Tilden Foundations)

CITY PLAY

When I was growing up before my family moved to another kind of neighborhood, we lived in a public housing project. It's a special something I think only Black people can really relate to. Projects were a part of every middle-income Black person's background at one point or another. My brother and I made very good friends with the family upstairs, with the children. During the summer, we would spend a lot of time in the bedroom singing, and the kids upstairs would be singing, too. We did four-part harmony through the ceilings, which were real thin. When our parents weren't there, we used the radiators for instrumentation. We used the radiators and spoons and the wooden beds and we'd sing and do harmony and have some background.[56]

In 1896, soon after the streets on the Lower East Side were paved, the *New York Tribune* published the article that follows, applauding the effects of paved streets on the play activities in the neighborhood; but the asphalt also put a halt to some bona fide New York traditions such as the election eve bonfire and children's games, such as mumblety peg and marbles, that required dirt.

> Asphalt pavements are an important contribution to the opportunities for amusement of the East Side. . . . It might appear that as the streets were there before, they would have served as well for playgrounds when paved with cobblestones, but such is not the case. Their superior cleanliness for one thing makes the asphalt pavements far more available. . . .
>
> The smoothness is perhaps the chief element in their adaptability to the sports of childhood. The boys can play marbles on them, while granite pavements are useless for this. It is lots more fun to roll a hoop, play ball or "one o' cat" or "prisoners' base" on asphalt than on rough stones, muddy, perhaps, and slippery. The little girls also find that "ring around a rosy" and other song games are much more satisfactorily played on a smooth surface. . . .
>
> The grown folk also reap benefits from the asphalt pavements. The children being on the street, there is more room on the sidewalk for their elders. Chairs are brought out on the sidewalk, and the curbstones furnish seats for many. With the old paving materials, the gutters were more or less unclean and noisome, but the asphalt makes the curbstone really an attractive place to sit.
>
> *New York Tribune,* July 5, 1896[58]

The Bouncing Ball

Consider the bouncing ball. Mapping out a game, a child must regard the way a ball will bounce against different surfaces. It matters if the block slopes up or down. Cracks on the sidewalk and uneven bricks offer a crazy, angled bounce. And every ball has its bounce quotient. "If a ball was dead," said Don Fellman,

Across the street there was a big apartment building and sitting in front of the apartment building every single day—in my memory I think of them being there always, even in the winter, although I'm sure they were not out in the winter—but in these kind of plastic folding chairs, the old Eastern European men and women would talk constantly in Yiddish about all of us in the neighborhood. We always joked that they knew everything that was going on. It was a sort of Greek chorus that commented on the morality of all of us.

Laura Simms, born 1947,
Borough Park, Brooklyn

The tragedy of losing your ball was that you had to ask your mother for a quarter and if you didn't have a ball no one would play with you.

Carole Baer, Yorkville, Manhattan,
and the Bronx

I lived in New York between 1971 and 1975, and I came here from Indiana which is where I grew up and basketball is just a big deal sport in Indiana. So when I came here it was quite jarring—I lived down on 17th Street in Lower Manhattan between 8th and 9th avenues, and we had a corner playground that had a hoop with no net, and in Indiana there was always nets on the hoops, but this was just an iron ring and all the players were city players and the rules were completely different.

The thing that always interested me and my friends from Indiana the most about it was the spatial quality of it. In Indiana, if you and I were playing each other and I shot the ball and missed and you got the rebound, you would have to clear the ball, throw the ball back below the free throw line. It replicates the space of having a full court. In Chelsea, New York, it's completely different. If I shoot the ball and I miss, and you get the rebound, you can shoot it right back up. It's condensed, it's all condensed. They even called the game "straight up."

And then in Indiana there's that aesthetic sort of sensual pleasure of having the ball rustle the net when it swishes through with backspin. [Here in New York there's just a big clang when the ball hits that metal hoop.] So in New York you don't find many outside shooters. The players that go to the pros and the college game from New York they're all great rebounders, but they can't shoot a lick. In Indiana, it's different—you don't get all these great rebounders but you get great pure shooters.

Phil Hoose, born 1947

"we had to 'roof it,' that is, get rid of it by heaving it onto a roof."[59]

Consider, too, the type of ball. Rubber balls bounce well against the concrete and asphalt of the streets and the brick walls of the city. The quintessential New York City ball was made from the inside of a tennis ball and was called a "spaldeen," a mispronunciation of its maker, the Spalding Company. These balls bounced high but they were soft enough that they did not easily break windows. The whiffle ball made of hard plastic with holes does not bounce as well: Bernard Mergen regards it as the quintessential suburban ball, ideal for play on lawns.[60] Richard Wallace talks about the uses of the "half ball" (literally a rubber ball sawn in half) in Philadelphia. Half balls were used in confined spaces, because they wouldn't travel far, and they provided the most unusual bounces. "The half ball would do things a whiffle ball wouldn't dream of."[61]

"The most common play object of today," writes Brian Sutton-Smith, "is the ball which is to the twentieth-century playground what the knife was to that of the nineteenth. Bitumen surfaces and asphalt playgrounds are too fast for marbles and too impregnable for stagknife, and they present an emotional barrier to games that require soft earth, dirt, and grass."[62] The ball be-

I can remember pink spaldeens—that was the ball you wanted to use for stoopball—pink spaldeens. It was right for the game. A golf ball would have been too springy and a tennis ball was not lively enough and there were solid foam balls which were a bit too heavy but the pink spaldeen was just right—it gave just the right degree of difficulty for the game.

Michael Kanarek, born 1948,
New Hyde Park, New York

Opposite: Street basketball, Lower East Side, Manhattan, 1978 (Photo © Martha Cooper/City Lore)

INCORPORATION

We played street football right there in the street. And this is where we had the greatest quarterback in the world. Our quarterback he had to control twenty-three men on each side, and he was really great at it. . . . Now here was a guy with an ingenious mind. He'd call a football play like this. He'd always get down on one knee and draw things. He'd take a Coke bottle top.

"Now, Shorty, this is you—this is a Coke bottle."

"I don't want to be the Coke bottle cap."

"What do you want to be?"

"I want to be the piece of glass."

"Now listen to this, now—Arnie, go down ten steps and cut left behind the black Chevy. Filbert, you run down to my house and wait in the living room. Cosby, you go down to 3rd Street, catch the J bus, have them open the door at 19th Street—I'll fake it to you."

There was always one fat kid you never thought of. "What about me?"

"You go long." We had a lot of good plays going back then.

Bill Cosby, born 1937, Philadelphia [63]

Game of marbles, 1914 (Photo from the Chicago Daily News, *courtesy of the* Chicago Historical Society)

CITY PLAY

came ubiquitous in the twentieth century—and it was ideal for playing on asphalt. Bouncing high, rolling fast, and easy to throw, the ball represents the increased "rate of play" on modern playgrounds, writes Sutton-Smith. "The swiftness and mobility of the ball as contrasted with stagknives, pocketknives, knucklebones, marbles, buttons, bells, caps, and tip cats is an index of the increase in playground speed."[64]

Skelly and Marbles

In *Letters to Phil: Memories of a New York Boyhood,* Gene Schermerhorn recalls that in the 1840s "marbles were played in a great ring four or five feet across marked out on the smooth, hard dirt; not in the miserable way they do now—a little spot of bare earth about two feet by four and three or four glass marbles, as I saw some boys playing the other day."[65] By the 1880s, children in New York already had a difficult time finding "good, clean dirt" for marbles (dirt was especially important for variations of marbles which shot the glass balls into a shallow hole called a "pot"); and by the early twentieth century the game was relegated to the strip of dirt between the street and sidewalk which children nicknamed the "boulevard." One New Yorker who grew up in the 1940s described how neighborhood children had to protect their one patch of dirt by trampling the shrubbery every time adults replanted it.

While marbles were not well adapted to asphalt and concrete, another old game was reinvigorated. Based on a game played with checkers (New Yorkers born in the first decade of this century still remember the original version), a new game called "skelly" (or "skelsies," "skully," "kilsies," "loadsies," "caps," "bottle caps," or "dead man," depending on the neighborhood) relied on bottle caps (and later, other kinds of plastic caps) as playing pieces. The pieces are flicked in a thumb and forefinger motion, and skim along the concrete into squares, usually

When I was a boy on 107th Street, we even chewed the tar on the streets. We lifted the top layer off then pulled pieces from below. There was even a myth that if you chewed some of that, it would clean your teeth. God knows, it was probably cancerous. . . .

The sidewalk was our sandpaper. If you rub a peach pit on its fat side, eventually you'll rub a hole through it. Then you'd clean out the hole with a penknife. You could mold the outer edges as well, and wear it as a ring or as a weapon.

Ed Brophy, born 1937,
Upper West Side, Manhattan

We were always searching for bottle caps to use in skelly games, and in the candy store at the top of the hill, there was this permanent bottle opener, and kids would come in and buy a bottle of orange soda, and the kids would use it, and there was a bin down there, and the syrupy soda would create this kind of odor that was very atmospheric like a movie theater, and the wood was stained, and old-looking. And there were phone booths next to that, and in the corner between the phone booths and the wall, I would notice a pile of bottle caps on the floor. They would take all different forms, many of them were bent from the opener, some of them almost came to a point, and I would find some there that were almost perfect—they looked like someone had just *lifted* them off. And I remember at one point Marvin and I racing to the candy store to get a crack at the lids, that was like another sport of ours. It was like a regular ritual.

Don Fellman, born 1949, Long Island City, Queens

INCORPORATION

EAST SIDE CHILDREN

Boys playing checkers, Lower East Side, Manhattan, late nineteenth century (Library of Congress)

We used crayons to weight the skelly caps, and I melted them in. I used a magnifying glass. At my window, I would take different color crayons, and affix the beam of light so they would melt and move and flow around—it was almost like a chemical experiment.

Don Fellman, born 1949, Long Island City, Queens

Election Eve and Election Day were big events in our neighborhood.

On Election Eve, a huge bonfire was ceremoniously lit on the corner of MacDougal Street and Saratoga Avenue. The kids would save pieces of wood for weeks before the event. My brother and I contributed the most because all canned and packaged goods came packed in wood and by Election Eve our cellar was nearly full of empty boxes and crates.

Most of the grownups and all of the kids would gather around the fire, whooping it up for their candidates, singing and generally making as much noise as possible.

The bonfires came to an end the year the street was paved. After the fire burned out, we discovered that it had melted a huge area in the middle of the intersection and from then on bonfires were banned.

William M. Firshing, born 1899, Bedford-Stuyvesant, Brooklyn [66]

Opposite: Boy melting wax for skelly cap, Bedford-Stuyvesant, Brooklyn, 1986 (Photo by Steven Zeitlin, Queens Council on the Arts)

CITY PLAY

Boy playing skelly, Sunnyside, Queens, 1985 (Photo by Steven Zeitlin, Queens Council on the Arts)

There were two kinds of playing pieces in our neighborhood. One was made from the corks used in liquor bottles. Back then the corks had a black, plastic piece to keep the cork in place. Boys would go into the garbage cans and search for those corks. They would cut the cork off and smooth it down by rubbing it on the sidewalk. The other playing piece was made from Coke bottle tops weighted with orange peels.

Lionel Senhouse, born 1933,
Brownsville, Brooklyn

numbered one to thirteen with a skull and crossbones drawn in the center (thus, we speculate, the name "skully" or "dead man").

Skelly boards are often drawn on the street next to the hydrant, the only curb space regularly free of cars. The caps, especially when weighted with tar, cork, pennies, melted crayons, orange peels, wax, or almost anything, skim nicely along concrete surfaces with the sideways flick of the finger—a well-weighted cap can be effective in knocking an opponent's caps off the board. Because the fingers flick sideways rather than up and down, players do not scrape their knuckles as they do trying to play marbles on asphalt and concrete; although marbles persisted, skelly prevailed.

Today, nostalgic marble sets packaged in old-fashioned wooden boxes by The Great American Marble Company and others are often sold in toy stores and museum shops. Perhaps marbles is a good game for playing on the surfaces where many contemporary play activities are centered—along the wall-to-wall carpets of today's living rooms.

In New York, where the Parks and Recreation Department prohibits skateboarding in parks and on playgrounds, many skateboard riders have found the area under the Brooklyn Bridge ramps on the Manhattan side to be the best arena. . . .

With a fairly smooth surface, many curbs to jump and several inclines good for stunts, the graffiti-covered banks below the bridge are ideal for daring riders. They even attract out-of-town skateboarders.

"This is better than any place in Philadelphia," said Roger Browne, 24, of Philadelphia, who comes to the area when he is in town. "All I do is go to work, sleep and ride my skateboard. This place is perfect for me."

New York Times, *July 30, 1989*[67]

Making One's Mark on the City

One of the ways for a child to lay claim to the environment is to write, carve, or paint a name on it. A logical progression leads from the stick, which enabled the child to draw in the dirt; to the knife, with which one could carve one's name on a tree or a school desk; to chalk, with which to put a name on a wall or a street; to a can of spray paint with which to make a mark on a subway car. From a child's perspective, placing one's name on any object confers a kind of ownership, and this is important for a child who may own very little except for a name.

In the 1960s, children at the Marcy Projects in Bedford-Stuyvesant, Brooklyn, and in other areas of the city developed "tag" or nicknames and began writing them on walls. The tag names hid their real identities from the authorities while still enabling them to communicate with each other. This, and the discovery of spray paint, led to the advent of graffiti, a game played by teenage city children for "fame." In New York, youngsters evolved a form of comic-strip train art which was celebrated in art galleries including the Bond Street Museum of Graffiti, and which became a central component of "hip-hop culture" and the wave of films and records it spawned. The artists and their communities, looking at the best examples of the tradition, regarded it as the visual component of hip-hop culture: "rap" was the music, "breaking" the dance, "graffiti" the visual art. One rapper describes scenes by the train yards, with the artists painting, the dancers breaking, and the singers rapping.[68] The city, looking at the worst examples of the tradition, considered the layers of scrawls on their trains a scourge and spent millions of dollars to eradicate them.

In every child's pocket there is a piece of chalk. And with this chalk he liberates his ideas and energies sketching upon the pavements intricate designs and forms which assist him in devising new games and aid him in keeping the old ones alive. Chalk games are among the most popular that children play and wherever one turns, on every city street, the unfailing patterns may be seen, which at night, after the children have retired from their play, resemble abandoned houses which once were full of the gusto of life.

Ethel and Oliver Hale, "From Sidewalk, Gutter, and Stoop."[69]

Skelly caps (Photo © Martha Cooper/ City Lore)

Chalk games, Prospect Place, Brooklyn, 1950 (Photo by Arthur Leipzig)

Beyond the Block

"We used to plan a trip to Chinatown to get firecrackers like someone would plan a trip to Europe. It was just loose talk and the plans would always dissolve."

DON FELLMAN, BORN 1949,
LONG ISLAND CITY, QUEENS

Each child had soda caps. You would have your own color wax you would melt into it. You knew who you were by the color your man was. I think I always was red. I love red.

Patricia Rutherford, born 1944, Brooklyn

As children grow older, they begin to explore beyond the block until the city itself becomes their field of play. "Yearly the circles of activity widen," wrote Michael Marks Davis in 1911, "the tot plays beside the family stoop, the little boy's range is his block, the older urchin scours the district, the young man travels about the city."[70] Writing about the same period, David Nasaw observes: "The bigger children as they approached their teens found the block too confining and the lure of foreign adventure too strong. In small groups or with their gangs, they searched the city for open space."[71]

The personal satisfactions to be won from an environment include the extent it can be used and manipulated. Young children and teenagers look at the urban landscape in terms of its potential for play. To what extent does it contain "useable rubbish, the detritus of packing cases, crates, bits of rope and old timber, off-

You just don't know how badly I want to reach my hands on a can of spray and touch my big train [that's] set in my yard and feel the voltage running through them trains while I paint my ghetto name on that iron screen for my people of the state of NYC to see and wonder on the art of the ghettos and the backstreets of our times.

Shy 147[72]

Boy painting a train in the yards, South Bronx, 1982 (Photo © Martha Cooper/ City Lore)

INCORPORATION

Painted train, South Bronx, 1982 (Photo © Martha Cooper/City Lore)

We used to take trips to the Silvercup Bakery and back. The bakery used to be right under the Queensborough Bridge—now it's a movie studio, but they kept that same huge sign which you can see as you come over the bridge. I would run into [my friend Dennis Burn] on the way over, and we'd turn that into a kind of game. One thing I did, there was a metal rod on the ground, and I would drag it along the cement on the side of the building and it would spark. The Silvercup Bakery was really a bread factory; Long Island City was very industrial then. And Dennis told me that they gave bread samples, little breads, he called them. So I went with him and there were Black workers there, and he had nicknames for them. One was called "Eye" because he had something wrong with his eye, the other was called "Face," because he told us to "get out of my face." Once we did get the sample breads and Dennis, on the way home—true to his street-kid spirit—waited for the right car to come along and threw the bread right under. When the car flattened it, it made a pop. That was his long-awaited thing. Ah, tales of Long Island City.

Don Fellman, born 1949, Long Island City, Queens

Opposite: Skateboarding in Riverside Park, Manhattan, 1979 (Photo © Len Speier)

My sister and I used to sneak into the Jewish synagogue near our apartment in the Bronx. Usually, the door was closed, but in the summer it was always open. We would hide in the pews and listen to the music. There was very low light and it sounded really haunted and spooky. My sister and I agreed it was even spookier than the Esperitismo Center my mother took us to on Tuesdays and Fridays.

Isabel Alvarez, born 1950, the Bronx

For a while I lived on 79th Street next to the Clifton which is still there only now it's a coop—but it used to be a hotel—and you know it's only a few steps from the back of the Museum of Natural History, and in the back there there was an area that I suppose used to be entered by horses and carriages, now cinder-blocked off—but at that time kids could sneak into those giant doors where they kept exhibits that were not being used. And we used to sneak in there and play—and my foster brother and I were in there one day with some of his pals, and we found this thing that I think must have been a replica of the Lincoln Memorial. And it looked like a statue of a man, and in the back there was a little door. So he went in there and he said, "Hey, there's light coming through his eyes! This is great! It's like a cave, you have to come in here."

So, of course I went in there and then he went out and shut the door and left me in there and he held it shut I guess 'cause I thought it was stuck or locked and he was gone, he was silent—first I was screaming for him and he didn't come. And then I had to make plans for surviving underneath— underneath the Museum of Natural History locked inside of a statue where nobody knew I was. But of course when I was quiet after a while, he finally thought I died and came to take the corpse out!

Susan Mildred Brown, 1940s and '50s,
Central Park South and West, Manhattan

Girls in the East River, Astoria, Queens, ca. 1940 (Fiorello La Guardia Memorial Archive)

CITY PLAY

cuts and old wheels?"[73] In what ways does it pose a challenge? Does it distinguish the "men from the boys," the girls from the boys, the brave from the faint-hearted? Is there refuse water to be rafted across? Are there junk piles and ledges worth being king of? Is there discarded wood that can be fashioned into a ramp for a bicycle or a skateboard? Is it dangerous but not foolhardy?

Rafting on the Hudson at 12th Street, Manhattan, 1930s (Photo by P. L. Sperr, Photographic Views of New York City, New York Public Library, Astor, Lenox, and Tilden Foundations)

The Rivers

Whether at the beach, a pool, in the rivers, or frozen in snow, water is a basic element of play and recreation. But it is deeply affected by the built environment which moves, pollutes, re-shapes, and builds around it.

For much of the city's history, swimming in the Hudson and East rivers were major forms of recreation. Today, even access to the waterways is closed off; construction has blocked most of the pathways to the river's edge. Fears about pollution have also kept youngsters from swimming in the rivers; today, a tetanus shot is required to participate in the annual swimming race around Manhattan Island! Often, we assume that the rivers were cleaner a generation ago—but, as our oral histories suggest, what may have changed is not the level of pollution but the level of concern.

When we were kids, we swam in the Hudson River in the area around Columbia University. The first one in had to splash his hands wildly to "break the shit line" and make way for the rest of us.

Ed Brophy, born 1937, Upper West Side, Manhattan

INCORPORATION

The East River was both our playground and our lifeline. We swam through the raw untreated garbage which was dumped regularly into the river. We dove off the cargo barges as they were being pulled toward shore, against the tide, by their little tugboats. Before I was out of my early teens I was swimming to Manhattan and back with such ease that on three separate occasions I was able to rescue friends of mine who couldn't make it. If I hadn't been such a powerful swimmer in my youth I would never have been able to save myself, years later, when an attempt to escape from a Pennsylvania prison through the main sewer went all wrong.

Willie Sutton, born 1901, Brooklyn [74]

The Kill Van Kull is the river that separates New Jersey from the north shore of Staten Island where I used to live. I lived two blocks from the river. I mean this was very rare—we didn't do this too often—my mother will kill me if she finds out—so anyway on a hot summer day, we went down to the river and jumped in. But there were rules—and the rules were that you never, ever put anything above your chin under the water. Now I don't know how you're going to describe this, but the Kill Van Kull Crawl required that you take a doggie paddle stroke with one hand and a surface breast stroke with the other, and in this way, you could make time on the first and push the shit aside on the second.

Roberta Singer, born 1941, Staten Island

In my day, the pastime called "Follow Master" was a decided favorite, particularly of boys. It was an exercise of high adventure and of thrills. I recall five or six boys strung out in Indian file behind an intrepid leader, imitating all his actions and his feats. Sometimes, we walked long distances, far beyond our neighborhoods, weaving in and out of pedestrians and of horse traffic. . . . Once we penetrated into territory leading onto a steel bridge flung across the Harlem River, and a single dare impelled our "Master" to climb up the superstructure, causing us to follow him, reluctantly enough, as though lured by some inevitable fate. I cannot recall how high we climbed but I remember ladders being raised and ourselves brought down amid deep voices and confusion; I should recall my father's punishment, but that escapes my memory.

Ethel and Oliver Hale, born 1891 and 1893, Harlem, Manhattan [75]

Opposite: Coney Island Polar Bear Club members, Brooklyn (Photo by Nancy Rudolph, Museum of the City of New York)

INCORPORATION

CITY PLAY

Snow and Sand

Sand and snow are the city's malleable surfaces; unlike asphalt and concrete, they can be manipulated, picked up, piled, shaped, thrown. Sand castles are sculpted from New York's sandy shoreline; mixing wet and soft sand, mudballs are rounded and pressed; children playfully bury themselves; names and messages are written with shells and sticks on the sand and washed away by the tide.

Snow is a seasonal transformation of the city's surfaces. Slopes that make ballgames difficult are ideal for sledding. Ponds used for fishing become skating rinks. Snow imparts a timeless quality to the urban landscape, softens its jagged edges. Traffic slows. Streetlights render the snow-coated trees iridescent. The urban landscape comes to resemble the streets of a small town.

Many New Yorkers talk about a childhood in which snow was more plentiful than it is today. This may have a basis in changing weather patterns; historically, too, snow was around much longer than it is today; snow removal was not as sophisticated, and a city with fewer "modern conveniences" generated less heat. But the seeming abundance of snow may also be memory's sleight of hand.

Sledding at the corner of Greenwich and Warren streets, Manhattan, 1809 (Watercolor, Baroness Hyde de Neuville Collection, Museum of the City of New York)

Opposite: Children swimming off Pierrepont Street, Brooklyn, ca. 1930 (Underwood and Underwood, Photographic Views of New York City, New York Public Library, Astor, Lenox, and Tilden Foundations)

INCORPORATION

Sleighing on Broadway, Manhattan, 1858 (Wood engraving, Museum of the City of New York)

January 23, 1887. It seems to me that we had a great deal more snow then [in the 1840s], than we have now: there used to be good sleighing in Broadway for weeks at a time, and all the stage lines ran huge open sleighs in place of the usual stages. . . .

In the evenings large parties would get on the sleighs and ride down to the South Ferry and back and oh! what fun: such shouting and snowballing and such good times generally.

The sleighs all had at least four horses and sometimes six, eight, or ten. I have known sixteen and twenty on some of the larger ones. People used to crowd in and hang on the outside, while there always seemed to be room for one more. Someone would shout, "Come right up here by the stove." Of course there was no stove but they would crowd up all the same. On the boxes were sometimes men dressed in fancy costumes of like old women. I remember once seeing some men with huge tin trumpets eight or ten feet long. Every small boy who could not ride, seemed to feel like taking it out on those who could by pelting them with snowballs, but no one seemed to mind it much.

Gene Schermerhorn, born 1842, Lower Manhattan[76]

CITY PLAY

My grandfather had ships that went to Holland and he brought skates home to his children, and they used to skate on the Canal that is now Canal Street and on the pond where the Tombs is now, and my mother says that the poor people used to get a rib of beef and polish it and drill holes in it and fasten it on their shoes to skate on.

Catherine Elizabeth Havens, born 1839, Brooklyn[77]

Sledding in Central Park, 1898 (Photo by Byron, Museum of the City of New York)

INCORPORATION

Rockaway, 1899 (Photo by Byron, Museum of the City of New York)

On weekdays only few, scattered groups of people, mainly women and children, were to be found along this vast stretch of beach [at Coney Island], and the only sound of which one was aware was the soft, incessant splash of waves as they rolled upon the sand. Here, in the clear, unpolluted air, on the clean, white sand, beneath the brilliant summer sunshine, I grew brown and ruddy and strong. Here with my little pail and shovel, that I prized as a king might prize his scepter and crown, I played through long, happy summer days, sometimes alone, but more often with other children who happened to be on the beach, and who mingled as freely and naturally as friendly puppies. We would make sand pies and decorate them with seaweeds and shells. We would pile up sand hills and dig tunnels through them. We would dig canals as the tide came in and watch the water run into them, and we would cover each other with sand up to our necks. The greatest joy was to take off our shoes and stockings and wade into the surf. Some youngsters barely wetted their feet and ran back screaming when a wave came toward them. But I always waded out until the rims of my petticoats became wet and mother called to me to come back. I was too familiar with the waves to fear them.

Meta Lilienthal, born 1876, Lower East Side, Manhattan[78]

Opposite: Children playing in the snow, Monroe Street, Lower East Side, 1947 (Photo by Rebecca Lepkoff)

Sledding in Central Park, 1985 (Photo © Martha Cooper/City Lore)

Our skates were a primitive instrument, compared with those of a later period. The blades were very thin, and generally of iron, involving the frequent filing of the gutters to keep them sufficiently sharp for safety; there were heel and toe straps, without screws for the heel of the shoe; and as a result, we had to draw all the straps so tight, to maintain the skates in position, that the necessary circulation of the blood in our feet was arrested, and we were frequently tortured with pain and cold.

Charles Haynes Haswell, born 1809, Manhattan [80]

Nature in the City

"Once," writes Michael Gold about his childhood at the turn-of-the-century on the Lower East Side, "Jake Gottlieb and I discovered grass struggling between the sidewalk cracks near the livery stable. We were amazed by this miracle. We guarded this treasure, allowed no one to step on it. Every hour the gang studied 'our' grass, to try to catch it growing. It died, of course, after a few days; only children are hardy enough to grow on the East Side." [79]

Despite the massive built environment, bits and pieces of nature do poke through sidewalks and city yards; children made a tradition of shaping rings out of peach pits and recall how they would squeeze and even blow up the rubbery jade leaves that jutted from the planters on either side of the front stoops. "We have only one tree on our block," a thirteen-year-old told us, "but we pretend it's a whole forest."

Beginning in the early nineteenth century, city planners, seeing nature vanishing under the cobblestones and brick, began planning city parks; Central Park was begun in 1853, Prospect in 1866. More recently, Flushing Meadow-Corona Park in

Opposite: Boy running in Central Park, 1953 (Photo by Arthur Leipzig)

INCORPORATION

Roller skater in Central Park, 1985 (Photo by Steven Zeitlin, Queens Council on the Arts)

CITY PLAY

Queens was developed on the site where two world's fairs were erected in 1939 and 1964.

The parks are a way of making the natural environment accessible to city children and adults. On a summer day in the crowded, concrete city of New York, people can go fishing, rock climbing, boating, and bird watching in Central Park; in the winter they go ice skating and cross-country skiing. In the park, a birder named Lambert Pohner claims to have seen more than two hundred species of birds.

"In a city where people can live 63,000 to a square mile," writes Donald Knowler, "Central Park represents the great escape. The Park may be one of the most trampled patches of greenery on earth but it still means freedom, a place for pleasure, a breathing space."[81] In New York, the parks represent not only a place where one can experience the sights and sounds and smells of nature, but a space where one can move through it, unencumbered by cars, traffic lights, and an array of other obstacles. Flushing Meadow-Corona Park in Queens, Crotona Park in the Bronx, Prospect Park in Brooklyn allow the same movement, but packed into mid and upper Manhattan, Central Park exudes this frenetic mood of escape, of freedom. Joggers run, bicyclists pedal furiously, roller skaters spin and turn. In a traffic-jammed, gridlocked town—where it is said that the shortest unit of measurable time is between the traffic lights turning green and the cars behind honking—unfettered locomotion on skateboards, bicycles, rowboats, or roller skates becomes a precious form of play.

Carlitos was the son of a friend of mine who I knew in Puerto Rico. Then they moved here and we reestablished contact. He was eight or nine, and I started to go over and visit with his parents, but I got to like the kid. I would visit with him a couple of days a week. He grew up near the sea in Puerto Rico. So what I saw was a kid in a little apartment where he couldn't make any noise because the people downstairs would complain. He wasn't a real street kid, and there were places where he couldn't play on the street—it was 110th Street and Fifth Avenue. There were prostitutes, and he was afraid he'd get hit by a bullet he wasn't meant for. Other kids adapted, they'd play among the drug dealers, or they'd play dope dealer, but he didn't aspire to that.

So I'd buy him a hot dog and take him to Central Park. And all he did was run, run, run. He was like a kid on a mission. We'd go to the Sheep Meadow, and he'd run in a particular way—and it seemed to me like the sky was real big and there's this little kid. It was like he was running through the air. It was beautiful.

You know the Meadow is flat—you can see the horizon, where the earth meets the sky. He had that all the time in Puerto Rico but in Manhattan, Sheep Meadow in the park is just about the only place you can see the horizon. I imagine that's what meant the most to him.

Raul Acero, born 1950, Bogota, Colombia, and Queens

INCORPORATION

CHAPTER

THREE

TRANSFORMATION

"And we mistake
the things we see
for what they are."

STEVEN SMITH,
BLIND ZONE[1]

Martha Cooper

Play is the process of creating a set of activities for pleasure based upon a set of rules and boundaries defined by the players themselves. Let this be first base—and so it is. Let this sidewalk square be jail, let this broken antenna be a ray gun—through the magic of play, it is. Transformation is the process of taking the rules, the boundaries, the images, the characters of the real world and recasting them within the boundaries of play. At the heart of play is this process of taking a given space or object and devising a new use for it, thereby making it one's own.

In 1952, anthropologist Gregory Bateson visited the San Fran-

Stickball game, East 184th Street, the Bronx, 1984 (Photo by Alan Zale, New York Times, *June 13, 1984)*

CITY PLAY

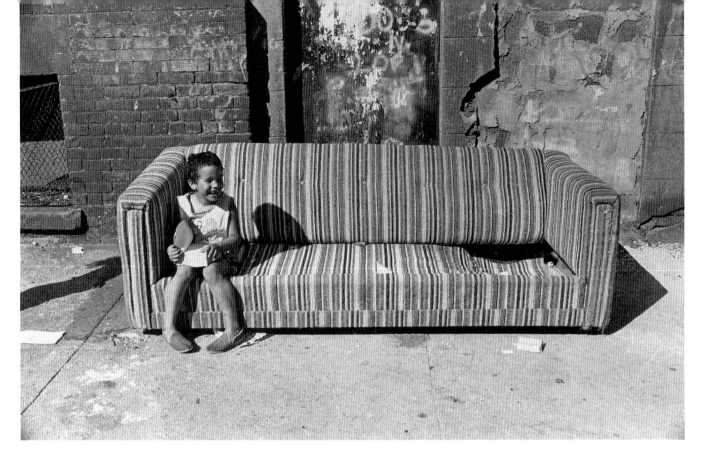

A dumped couch . . .

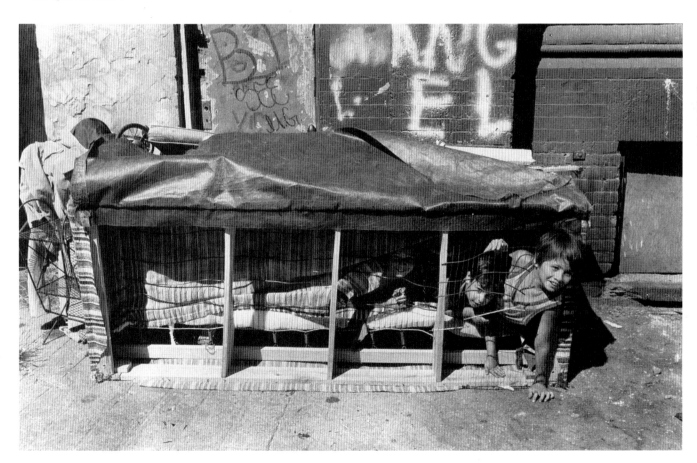

. . . becomes a clubhouse, Lower East Side, Manhattan, 1978 (Photos © Martha Cooper/City Lore)

cisco Zoo, where he observed two monkeys playing. They were playfully nipping at one another, not biting. Bateson realized that this could only have occurred if at some point the monkeys had exchanged the message, "This is play." His observation became the basis for an important kind of anthropological analysis; many kinds of human messages are "framed" and interpreted not according to their literal referents but according to a set of agreed-upon meanings.[2] For children, the message "this is play" transforms the significance of all the objects manipulated, the settings acted upon, and the actions which transpire before their mother calls them in for dinner, the school bell rings, or some other signal indicates, "this is no longer play." At that point, the "Johnny pump" becomes a hydrant, the shield a garbage can lid again.

Opposite: Boy with stick, Lower East Side, Manhattan, 1978 (Photo © Martha Cooper/City Lore)

Fifth Avenue parade re-created in Sunnyside, Queens, 1985 (Photo by Steven Zeitlin, Queens Council on the Arts)

One of my friends, Marvin Schwartz, would give us flying lessons on the benches in our projects. They consisted of lying on the flat benches and, with the arms outstretched, making air sounds like a reverse vacuum cleaner.

Don Fellman, born 1949,
Long Island City, Queens

TRANSFORMATION

"I can fly," one of the children called out from a vestibule, and showed us. Standing in the doorway, she pressed each side of it with both hands as hard as she could and then turned sideways. Her arms, released from the outward pressure, lifted a bit, involuntarily, and she called this flying. She explained that a brother had shown her this feat, and she was very proud of it, repeating it several times as if it had been her original idea. . . .

. . . We have seen children play, pretend and imagine, excellent actors indeed, and one day, passing a little group, saw them jump rope having no rope at all. We stopped and listened to them a long while and saw them pretend that the separating cracks between two flagstones was the turning rope that must be cleared. It was a serious pretense, actually, to them; the rope was there and the crack, under the children's feet like a river being spanned, contained all the hazards of the turning thing.

Ethel and Oliver Hale, "From Sidewalk, Gutter, and Stoop."[4]

As they transform the city for play, New Yorkers manifest a remarkable imagination. The contours of the city, with its hydrants, curbs, and cornices, become the gameboard. The castoffs of city living—bottle caps, broomsticks, and tin cans—become the pieces on the board. A playful order of things prevails. People are at their most revealing when they take themselves least seriously.[3]

Junk into Toys

"The streets may not have been paved with gold, but they were littered with junk."

DAVID NASAW, *CHILDREN OF THE CITY*[5]

"The older kids," writes humorist Sam Levenson, "taught the younger ones the arts and crafts of the street." Growing up in an East Harlem tenement, he recalls how "ashcan covers were converted into Roman shields, oatmeal boxes into telephones, combs covered with tissue paper into kazoos . . . a chicken gullet into Robin Hood's horn, candlesticks into trumpets, orange crates into store counters, peanuts into earrings, hatboxes into drums, clothespins into pistols, and lumps of sugar into dice."[6]

Street toys are made not simply from "found" objects but from "searched for" objects; often a great deal of effort goes into locating precisely the right objects for play. In Bedford-Stuyvesant, for instance, prized skelly caps were fashioned by filing a Moosehead Ale bottleneck on the curb to produce a glass ring smooth enough to glide along concrete. In Astoria, the best skelly pieces were the plastic caps on the feet of school desks.[7] In many neighborhoods, "swiping" the parts for toys enhanced their value. According to a "writer" named "Sach," true graffiti can be executed only with stolen cans of paint.[8]

Walking sticks, Lower East Side, Manhattan, 1978 (Photo © Martha Cooper/ City Lore)

Boy with toy gun, Williamsburg, Brooklyn, 1986 (Photo © Martha Cooper/ City Lore)

Different neighborhoods provide their own raw materials. In Chinatown, mothers who work in the garment industry provide the sought-after items. Jacks are often made from buttons— each "button jack" consists of a set of five or six buttons sewn together. Children use rubberbands hooked together to create a "Chinese jump rope."[9] The elastic is stretched between the feet of two girls while a third does cat's cradle–like stunts with her legs. Sometimes, the ropes are fashioned from white elastic bands which mothers bring home from the factories.

In America today, adult toymakers working for large companies masterfully manufacture an endless variety of toys for children. They clearly understand the child's fascination with transformations; many of their toys are open-ended, devised to be used in different ways. In the 1980s, toymakers at Mattel actually named a set of toys with an accompanying television program "Transformers"—plastic robots that with a series of clever twists become cars, tanks, rocketships, and airplanes. Their slogan is, "Transformers—more than meets the eye." These new, not inexpensive but ubiquitous toys with their bright colors and slick plastic surfaces texture the world of the contemporary American child.

Bean shooters, Lower East Side, Manhattan, 1979 (Photo © Martha Cooper/ City Lore)

TRANSFORMATION

Some adults, however, continue to make toys for their children and grandchildren. Since many manufactured toys are inexpensive, handcrafted items require a self-conscious effort, but have a noncommercial character that carries a personal touch. The self-styled toymakers are often trying to teach a new generation about their own childhood when homemade toys were all they had. At one point, Henry Callejo of Astoria, Queens, saw his grandson discarding some used kitchen matches. He asked him to bring over the matches and explained to him how some-

Go-cart made from shoebox, New York City, 1912 (Bain Collection, Library of Congress)

Opposite: Pushmobile, Brooklyn, 1943 (Photo by Arthur Leipzig)

TRANSFORMATION

thing as simple as a match might mean to a small child in Italy half a century ago; Callejo made a miniature house of matchsticks to demonstrate the importance of conservation.[10]

Immigrants from the rural areas of Puerto Rico have a strong tradition of making toys from found objects. Pablo Falcon, a retired carpenter, uses the detritus of urban life—discarded sardine cans, bottles, bottle caps, plastic medicine bottles—to handcraft toys which, ironically, teach his grandchildren about his rural childhood. They show Puerto Rican children raised in Brooklyn the kinds of Christmas presents their parents once received on the island during Three Kings Day, when people had

Go-cart race, Lower East Side, Manhattan, 1978 (Photo © Martha Cooper/ City Lore)

CITY PLAY

little money, but had the time and skill to make beautiful toys from the materials at hand.[11] The toys are multivocal in their symbolism; depicting actual scenes from the past, they teach about countries, eras, and events; but they also suggest the importance of conserving the physical environment, and preserving a cultural heritage.

Street television, Lower East Side, Manhattan, 1979 (Photo © Martha Cooper/ City Lore)

In the 1930s and '40s, we used to make "pushmobiles" out of an orange crate and an old skate. That was a basic New York City street toy. We really used to race these things. They were our racing machines, everyone had his own tune he'd sing when racing downhill—mine was the theme from the Lone Ranger.

[And] we used to make fedora beanies out of men's fedora hats. Every man wore a fedora hat in those days, so usually they were easy to come by. But if we couldn't find one, what we did was go down to the subway on those hot summer days when the windows were open on the trains. You'd stand on the platform near an open window and just as the train was leaving you'd gently lift the hat from a man's head.

Ed Brophy, born 1937, Upper West Side, Manhattan[12]

TRANSFORMATION

If a baseball was required, a boy of 1816 founded it with a bit of cork, or, if he were singularly fortunate, with some shreds of india-rubber; then it was wound with yarn from a ravelled stocking, and some feminine member of his family covered it with patches from a soiled glove. . . . Their footballs were made with a bladder purchased from a butcher and covered by a neighboring shoemaker.

Charles Haynes Haswell,
born 1809, Manhattan [13]

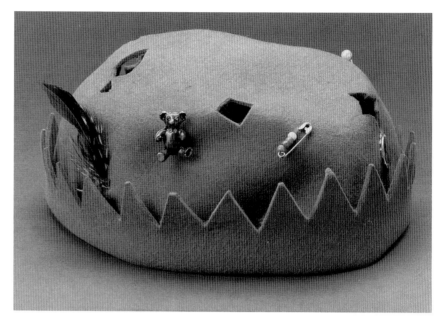

Fedora beanie made by Ed Brophy (Photo © Martha Cooper/City Lore)

Re-creation of a "Depression football," made of newspaper by Robert Burghardt (Photo © Martha Cooper/City Lore)

CITY PLAY

Manuel Perez of Staten Island made this beautiful carousel out of an old broom-handle and pieces of tin, 1987 (Photo © Martha Cooper/City Lore)

I make kites out of plastic garbage bags with my mother. My grandmother always made kites for me too in Hong Kong. She used colorful plastic bags. My uncle worked in the store and there were a lot of large and colorful plastic [bags]. Sometimes my big brother would go with me to get bamboo sticks in the forest. He had an axe to chop them off because I was too little. Once my grandmother made a dragon with thirteen pieces. My great-grandmother taught her.

Ann Ng, 1970s and '80s, Hong Kong and Chinatown, Manhattan

"Oscar lived just off Lexington. He was disabled, had no legs, and he lived on the top of a six-floor walkup. He made carpet guns and used to have a call box hanging down to the sidewalk. If you wanted a gun you'd call up and he'd send a gun down in a bucket. Then you'd put twenty-five cents in the bucket and he'd haul it up."

"Were carpet guns the same as linoleum guns?"

"In our neighborhood, linoleum was carpeting."

Dominick Schillizi, born 1937, East Harlem, Manhattan

TRANSFORMATION

Every type of kid could get fireworks except me, and any firecracker I found in the street was so treasured I didn't even want to shoot it off. I used to try to make my own. The closest thing to an explosive I had access to was the sulfur tips of matches, so I took some matches out of a matchbook and I started to scrape the sulfur. Then I developed a system for removing the heads and the sulfur, and then I would wrap the heads and make a fuse. And I took this downstairs on one overcast day, and there wasn't much of anyone outside, just some younger Hispanic kid playing by the barrels. I told him, I got this bomb here and I was going to light it, and I got it into the barrel, which was good because it would shield the wind, and I tried out the bomb. And it looked like when a matchbook goes up, so it was a little disappointing but there was an element of pretend in it.

So then I was up at Michael's and happened to tell him about this and he was getting interested. So next thing I know, I'm making bombs for the Big Cheese. And he would bring matchbooks to me and I would twist the heads—so my position was going up from court jester to alchemist. I was gaining in rank.

Don Fellman, born 1949, Long Island City, Queens

Pretending and Dressing Up

"Ain't it funny how an old broken bottle
Can look just like a diamond ring."

JOHN PRINE, "FAR FROM ME" [14]

City children, like their rural and suburban counterparts, mimic the adult world around them. In Sunnyside, Queens, we have watched the local children transform the narrow back alley into their version of Fifth Avenue; the children hail taxis and merrily mimic the St. Patrick's Day and Macy's Thanksgiving parades. In other neighborhoods, children play priest, gas station attendant, pet store owner, baby, doctor, and even drug dealer (see Afterword).

By donning pieces of the city as rings or glittering jewelry, children appropriate adult notions of value and beauty. Girls (and sometimes boys) fashion jewelry out of urban debris. Gum wrapper necklaces, paper clip bracelets, and peach pit rings become part of many city girls' wardrobes.

Dramatic play, with its emphasis on the imagination, is as comfortable in the home as on the street; it takes place indoors or outdoors depending on the weather and the season and the safety of the neighborhood. "From the child's perspective the house is a rich play environment," writes Bernard Mergen. "Floors, carpeted and bare, provide that basic surface for playing with marbles, toys and blocks or for spreading things out to see how they look. Furniture can be easily incorporated into a play

Fighting the battles of World War I on the lawns of Queens (Family photo, Richard Crum)

My sister and I used to play in the house on Saturday morning because girls weren't allowed to go out as much. And she's the one who said, "You know, there's a city behind the television." See, these old televisions used to have the cardboard [backs] with holes in them. The television was on and we could see all of the lights on in the back. I remember the structure: there were big tubes on the left and big tubes on the right and these tiny tubes in the middle. So we took the cardboard off and put our dolls in there and played that it was the city of Manhattan. It was our own doll's house.

Isabel Alvarez, born 1950, the Bronx

I was a boy of ten during World War I. The enthusiasm for that misbegotten enterprise in our town, as elsewhere, surpasses belief. Afternoons and evenings, entertainment and all manner of goodies were dispensed (free, of course) to soldiers on leave from Camp Mills (out Mineola way) or the more distant Camp Upton. These men flowed into Jamaica in vast numbers during the war years. We kids assailed them constantly for "an extra button," which they would often reach into their pockets and produce: Symbols on them indicated the branch of service, sometimes the company number. Most prized were buttons from the Tank Corps (new then) and shoulder insignia (cloth) of the 77th (N.Y.) Division (Statue of Liberty) and the so-called Wildcat Division (khaki and crimson).

Patriotism was a continuing game to us kids of Eastwood—every day we played army with wooden guns or pop guns. We had wonderful dugouts descended to by an iron ladder, paved with ferns and roofed over by wooden slabs supported in the middle by an old railroad-tie. One boy had a real U.S. Army helmet, another had somehow acquired a spiked German helmet. I have a photo of one group so clad holding another group so clad at gunpoint.

Dr. Richard Crum, born 1907, Jamaica, Queens

TRANSFORMATION

One of the amusements at Rutgers Place was dressing up in various characters and making use of old-time costumes, brocade coats of our grandfathers and military equipments as both Uncle Rutgers and Grand-father Crosby were officers in the Revolutionary army. . . . [We also wore] the sash and sword worn by my father when a major in the War of 1812. . . . Then my mother had pre-served various bonnets of different fashions from extremely large to the extremely small, the high top and the poke, these always created great amusement.

Mary Crosby, born 1822,
Rutgers Place, Manhattan [17]

First high heels, Lower Manhattan, ca. 1951 (Photo by Jack Manning)

CITY PLAY

I don't think grown up people understand what children like—we love to dress up in long frocks and I guess all little girls like to, for my mother did. When she was about twelve years old she put on her mother's black lace shawl and walked out on Broadway in it, and her cousin, Katy Lawrence, met her in front of St. Paul's Church and saw the shawl dragging on the sidewalk and my mother looking behind to see if it dragged and she told my grandmother about it and my mother was punished. I know it was wrong but it must have been lovely to think that it really dragged and that people were looking at it. I'm afraid that I should have forgotten it was wrong.

Catherine Elizabeth Havens, born 1839, Brooklyn [15]

setting. Closets and cupboards become secret spaces within spaces. Fantasy and make-believe play can develop uninterrupted indoors." [16] Partly because of real and perceived dangers of the street, children in the city today spend more time playing indoors than their earlier counterparts. In our home in Sunnyside, Queens, for example, our children map a complex geography using the various surfaces of the house: floors become oceans, carpets and beds become continents and islands, and small throw rugs are used as boats to travel between them.

History on a grand scale has always provided scenarios for children's play in the city. Dressing up in Revolutionary War outfits, fighting the battles of World War I on the vacant lots of Queens, or holding two fingers under one's nose in the form of a mustache and jumping in a pool shouting "Heil Hitler," children imitate the great events of history. [18] Children at play write their own American history, a topsy-turvy parody of the ideas and the weapons and the battle cries of grown men who march out onto the battlefield and fight their wars like so many toy soldiers. Wars and battles provide grist for the next generation's childhood fantasies; real life is a wonderful storybook for children.

While dressing up and acting out different roles are part of a child's daily life, they formally dress up with adult supervision and encouragement on particular social occasions such as Halloween (earlier in the century, trick-or-treating was called "begging" and was done on Thanksgiving in New York). The festival of Purim in early spring is an occasion for Jewish children to dress up as biblical heroes or figures from popular culture. Hasidic children from the neighborhoods of Williamsburg and Borough Park, on this one day a year, have been observed dressing up as their Puerto Rican neighbors, carrying cardboard replicas of boom box radios. [19]

On certain sanctioned occasions, adults themselves will dress up. Masquerade balls and parades where adults dress in costume have a long history in the city. Recent immigrants have added their own masquerading traditions such as the West Indian Carnival, which annually parades along Eastern Parkway

Playing bartender . . .

in Brooklyn showing off brightly colored, phantasmagoric costumes that take a full year to create. Another recent tradition is the Greenwich Village Halloween parade, which transforms the narrow winding streets of the Village each October. Started by sculptor and puppet-maker Ralph Lee, the parade is influenced by Pop Art, street theater, and transvestite traditions in the city. Some revelers parody historic events—in 1988, two schoolteachers dressed as one of Imelda Marcos's famed pairs of shoes! Often people take the city as their theme, people dressing up as famous skyscrapers and landmarks, such as the Chrysler Building and the Statue of Liberty.[20] They have also been observed dressing up as the subways, as the Long Island Railroad, and as the corner of 5th Avenue and 59th Street. In 1988, the year the Williamsburg Bridge between Brooklyn and Manhattan was closed for drastic repairs, a group of friends recreated the suspension bridge and marched it along the parade route. These playful exercises, Kirshenblatt-Gimblett suggests, are a mapping of the city onto the human body.[21]

When I grow up I'm going to be a skier in the Olympics, but the whole time I'm a kid I want to be an explorer. I explore the park for dinosaur bones. One time I found one. It was real tiny. They don't call them dinosaur bones any more—they call them fossils. I'm still searching for the ancient steps in the park. Alissa told me about them. They're near the gate where the Lowers [lower playground] are. We think they might lead to diamonds, mummies, dead Indians, dead Pilgrims, and dinosaur bones. You have to dig two feet to get to them. When we get onto that subject, Alissa always gets greedy. She says if we find them we should give all the Indian stuff to her, and I could have anything else. But I told her that if I found Indian stuff I would keep it, and if she found it she could keep it. I found an Indian instrument today. . . .

Another thing I discovered was a no-gravity rock. A no-gravity rock is very very small, it's so small no gravity can hit it. When you put it on the ground, it flies up. They're very very hard to find. Most of them are buried even deeper than China.

Benjamin Zeitlin, age four, born 1982, Sunnyside, Queens

TRANSFORMATION

*Sweeping dirt under the rug, Lower East Side, Manhattan, 1979 (Photo ©
Martha Cooper/City Lore)*

Cooking with dirt, Lower East Side, Manhattan, 1979 (Photo © Martha Cooper/ City Lore)

Doing the wash, Sunnyside, Queens, 1987 (Photo by Amanda Dargan, Queens Council on the Arts)

We had given each of the children a few cherries. One of them found two whose stems were joined together. She placed the double stem over an ear and the two purple spheres hung from it. "Look at my earring," she said, and was very proud of it, feeling, no doubt somewhat like a gypsy or like a grownup at any rate.

Ethel and Oliver Hale, "From Sidewalk, Gutter, and Stoop."[22]

Playing baby, Lower East Side, Manhattan, 1978 (Photo © Martha Cooper/ City Lore)

I think it was 1953 or 1954—it was the summer when there was a big polio scare, and my mother told me two things about mud in the beginning of the summer—and the first was that I should not play in the mud because it was believed that children got polio from playing in the mud, and actually as kids we always did play in the mud in the backyard. But the second thing that she told me one day, not related to this at all, was sitting on the back porch and looking out into the garden there was an area I'm not quite sure why but nothing ever grew—everything else grew verdantly but in that part of the garden nothing grew so it was always murky and muddy and my mother told me that if you dug right through the mud in that part of the garden, that eventually you'd come to China. And China, of course, was a very big part of our lives because anything that you didn't eat went to China. . . .

So one day in the summer, Leah and Phyllis [my two best friends] and I went out to dig for treasure and we dug and we dug and we dug and we didn't find anything and we kept digging much deeper than usual because we had nothing else to do. . . .

And we dug and we dug until for us there was a veritable mountain of dirt, and we didn't find any . . . treasure but what we did come across was mud—there was getting to be almost a little pool of mud now in the hole—and I knew there was something very important about mud—but I couldn't remember what it was.

And then I remembered that actually if we kept digging that we would get to China. So I told my friends, and they were also excited because they also knew that the food on their table went to China. So we kept digging now and we went on and dug and dug and dug until there was a pool—an ocean of water. And then, we were convinced that we were really getting close to China, but that actually we had come to the ocean.

And I think it was me who had the idea . . . that we should strip naked and cover ourselves from toe to head with mud. They loved the idea. So we took off our clothing—everything—and we folded it under the cherry tree [in Leah's backyard], and then we helped each other and we covered ourselves completely in mud, certain that not only would we not be recognized but we would hardly be known as human beings. And we invented a song called the mud sisters song, which went just like,

> We are the mud sisters
> Mud sisters, mud sisters, mud sisters.

And we decided to go out into the neighborhood, ring doorbells, sing our song and run away. . . .

But what I do remember was actually coming down the street with Leah and Phyllis and we were very happy and we were singing our song walking down the street—when I looked up and saw my mother and father standing in front of the house, and Phyllis and Leah's mother and father standing in front of the house. And then I had two blazing realizations. And one was that I remembered why I was not supposed to play in the mud, and the second one was that I looked down and realized that the mud on the three of us had long since melted and was gone and we were just completely stark naked on 47th Street [in Brooklyn].

TRANSFORMATION

I actually don't remember what my parents said to me—I have just pushed that out of my mind, but what I remembered next was standing in my backyard and my mother was holding my shoulders down, and I was again still stark naked. And she said to me, "Laura darling, this is going to hurt me more than it's going to hurt you." And looking up and seeing my father coming out the back door with just an enormous pot of scalding hot water. He poured the water from the porch over me, and my mother was scrubbing me with a scrubbing brush for fear that I would get polio, and I was screaming and crying as if I was being tortured alive. And then I suddenly I heard two other children being tortured by their parents, and [then] I caught my mother's eye, and actually we burst out laughing. . . . The absurdity of it really hit me. . . .

Actually, we didn't play in the mud anymore that summer. But what we did do, which I remember very vividly, was sit often at twilight underneath the cherry tree, and we would talk endlessly about what we would have done if we had just spent a little while longer digging and had actually gone to China.

Laura Simms, born 1947, Borough Park, Brooklyn

CITY PLAY

I used to build altars when I was young. My brothers and sisters used to think I was crazy. I would get different various boxes and make graduated altars, and get my grandmother's linen handkerchiefs and pin them on and then get little flowers into vases and put them on the side. And friends of mine who were altar boys used to get hosts from the priest. The hosts were not good after a while and the priest would just give them to us. We also said mass on washing machines—we used to drop a cloth over the machine, and while the machine was going say mass. We'd pretend some water was wine and have somebody be the priest.
Contributed anonymously, Brooklyn [23]

Dressing as the corner of 59th Street and Fifth Avenue, Halloween parade, Greenwich Village, Manhattan, 1984 (Photo © Martha Cooper/City Lore)

Opposite: Roach Motel, Halloween parade, Greenwich Village, Manhattan, 1984 (Photo © Martha Cooper/City Lore)

TRANSFORMATION

Winner of the 1988 Roseland Easter Bonnet Contest, Manhattan (Photo by Elaine Norman)

Horror movies really influenced us—we would have Monster Quizzes. We always began by saying, "comedy, drama or melodrama"—melodrama was a word I picked up from *TV Guide*—they would never say horror—they'd say melodrama. The quizzes always took place in a particular part of the projects where there was this slablike grate that heat comes out of. If we were doing a mummy movie, for instance, that would be the slab that the mummy was on—I was the mummy and Michael Marasa would be the archaeologist; Albert's specialty was to do the phantom. It was a pantomime quiz—you had your guys on the bench, and you had your guys standing up. In the film, he takes the mummy's pulse and finds that he has one—and then the mummy goes for the archaeologist's throat and sits up on the slab. We would decide among ourselves on the film, and we would look around for a prop, maybe there was a broken umbrella or a bird cage in the bushes. The bigger person would always be the monster and the smaller guy would be the human being—like with basketball, there's a height advantage.

Don Fellman, born 1949, Long Island City, Queens

CITY PLAY

Easter bonnet, Easter Parade, Fifth Avenue, Manhattan, 1988 (Photo by Elaine Norman)

TRANSFORMATION

C H A P T E R

F O U R

CONTROL

"For me, play is what a person does when he can choose the arbitrariness of the constraints within which he will act or imagine."

BRIAN SUTTON-SMITH [1]

Katrina Thomas

I n a crowded city with its contested arenas, the freedom to play is hardly regarded as a basic human right. In some parts of the city where space is uncontested, a child can mark the boundaries of a play space with a piece of chalk, nothing more is needed; children can "frame" their play spaces with boundaries based on mutual agreement. More often, however, the task of establishing play spaces takes on a different character as young and old battle for autonomy and control. Perhaps the toughness sometimes perceived in city children comes not from the imposing, rigid, physical environment which they must incorporate and transform in order to play, but from the human battles they must fight to control urban spaces, to earn and maintain the right playfully to transform some autonomous space in the city.

In this chapter, we chart the struggles of New Yorkers to locate and defend play spaces. We begin with the search for privacy and autonomy in urban clubhouses, moving then to the different kinds of battles fought over turf, showing first how battlelines are drawn between young gangs, then between young people and perhaps their most insidious enemy, the automobile; finally between young people and the urban reformers who seek to domesticate their games and uplift their play activities. Through it all, children strive to gain control over their play worlds. As Alissa Duffy chanted as she and a friend jumped up and down on a discarded refrigerator box, "We're just kids! I am five and he is three and we rule everything!"[2]

This was a time when cars were starting to become common in the Bronx. In the early years, in the '20s and the early '30s, there were some cars around, but they didn't occupy the whole street. We could play immies, we could count on vacant spaces between cars, big distances between cars. But they were coming in faster now, and our neighborhood somehow was picked to have a streetlight. They had installed the light fixture but the electricity had not been put on. So there was one summer where this stoplight was on the corner with no electricity. I don't know how it happened but somehow we came up with the idea of taking a mirror and reflecting the sun on to the stoplight so that [it] lit up by reflected light. And you could focus the reflection on to the red, you could focus it on to the green and we did that and we had the traffic under our control. And we thought this was the funniest, this was the greatest because we had all these cars stop and go at our doing. It made us feel just superb. We did it for hours and hours, and each one of us took turns controlling the cars and sometimes we'd keep them there for five minutes, and see the drivers get all frustrated and finally cross the red light. . . . This was the beginnings of our growing up and learning to control a situation. Up until then we were kids and we were controlled. And here as teenagers and preteenagers we had control and that made us feel great.

Julius Sokolsky, born 1925, the Bronx[3]

Opposite: King of the hill, Brooklyn, 1950 (Photo by Arthur Leipzig)

CONTROL

Defining Private Places

All of play is an effort to establish boundaries within which a certain set of rules applies; the clubhouse is an effort to make those boundaries real.

Within clubhouse walls, the most ordinary activities take on special meaning. Susan Mildred Brown talks about the effort required to get up into her childhood clubhouse above the elevator shaft of a Central Park South apartment, scrabbling up a sharp incline and duck-walking on the walls. What did she and her friends do when they finally settled into that dark alcove, where only a child could maneuver?

Clubhouse, Lower East Side, Manhattan, 1978 (Photo © Martha Cooper/ City Lore)

CITY PLAY

"We ate Fig Newtons and read comics," she told us.[4] But in that sanctified space these activities took on special meaning.

The urge to create clubhouses spans the life cycle; all over the city children create hideouts in nooks and crannies while adults are more formal in their arrangements. Finding space for clubs and leisure activities in a dense city environment is no simple task; many adult and young adult groups strive for a storefront, but few can afford that luxury; sometimes they achieve a second-story clubhouse, such as the Tirana Social Club on Allen Street where old men play cards and socialize. But more often they must settle for attics and cellars and vacant lots.

The Brooklyn Elite Checker Club is comprised of elderly Black men born in the South who did acquire a storefront clubhouse for their checker games in Bedford-Stuyvesant, Brooklyn, in the early '80s.[5] Unfortunately, a wrecking ball demolishing an adjacent structure came through the window of the club. Today, members are engaged in a legal struggle with the city to reinstate their clubhouse, but they continue to meet on park benches, and tell stories about where they were when the wrecking ball came through the window. They still adhere to their motto—"Win like

Clubhouse exterior . . .

CONTROL

Clubhouse interior, boys cooking with leaves, Lower East Side, Manhattan, 1978 (Photos © Martha Cooper/City Lore)

a champion, lose like a gentleman." The Brooklyn Elite is a telling example of an urban storefront club struggling to maintain play space in a city with spiraling real estate values.

Immigrants often organize themselves around ethnic social clubs which bring together residents of the same village in Greece or Italy, Eastern Europe or Puerto Rico, in basements and storefronts in the five boroughs of New York. These ethnic associations rise and fall and rise again each day in New York City, as immigrant groups arrive in this country, band together for support, and try to maintain continuity with their past as they chart strategies for success in America. Often these clubs perpetuate the play activities that thrived in Old World villages; in a number of cases the games they play, laden with symbolic associations to the home country, become more popular here than they ever were in their native land. The game of *kazanti*, for instance, a rudimentary predecessor of pinball used for gambling, was trundled through Cypriot villages on a wheelbarrow for festive occasions a generation ago. It was resurrected by the

Cypriot men's club in Astoria, Queens, and now plays a part in the annual Cypriot celebrations.

"In East Harlem and the South Bronx," writes Barbara Kirshenblatt-Gimblett, "little country cabins pop up incongruously on vacant lots between tenements and brownstones, some abandoned and others still intact. These old-fashioned *casitas*, once common in the Puerto Rican countryside, are now scattered throughout inner city neighborhoods, where vacant lots abound and where local men can no longer afford to rent space for their social clubs."[6] One *casita* member jokingly referred to his structure as "the millionaire's club."[7] Another told us, "Every time somebody makes money in the dice game, he buys a chicken or a goose and we take care of it here."[8]

"Brightly painted and rich in pastoral imagery, these little

The Brooklyn Elite Checker Club, 1980s (Photo by Susan Slyomovics)

CONTROL

Card players at Ecuadoran Social Club, Long Island City, Queens, 1985 (Photo © Martha Cooper/City Lore)

Jewish women playing mah-jong, Rockaway, Queens, 1984 (Photo © Martha Cooper/City Lore)

Casita, the Bronx, 1985 (Photo © Martha Cooper/City Lore)

cottages re-create in loving detail the veranda, wood-burning stove, latrine, chicken coop (complete with chickens), well, and gardens remembered from the Puerto Rican countryside."[9] In a testament to the transformative power of memory, one visitor to the rustic outhouse of Villa Puerto Rico, a *casita* in the Bronx, commented on the powerful odor: "When I went in there, it was like going back in time."[10]

"One *casita* was built by unemployed men, who salvaged materials from abandoned buildings nearby. Another was constructed by a retired carpenter on a parking lot. In one case, the city cooperated by clearing garbage from the lot and furnishing some garden supplies. . . . Men who are unemployed, retired, or marginally employed take pride in their ability to construct these

CONTROL

All the people know the place you have to go to play [the cockfight]. We go all together, we go in the basement, we start fighting. We can start at ten o'clock, and we finish the next morning at seven o'clock. That's the way we do it, because we Spanish, we born in Puerto Rico, and we love that over there. My father used to do it, my brother, my uncle. If your rooster's good, and mine is good, we can make a fight with five, ten thousand dollars. . . . We match them, in the same height, in the same weight. Then you put . . . on the spur, and then we tape it all around. That's the point that they kill with. In Spanish, *espuela.* They make it out of the fish in the sea, the big one. It's a tail bone. And for that *espuela,* you can pay five hundred dollars for one pair. . . .

When they start fighting, they start jumping, you know. If you know about rooster, you know when he throw his leg and he hit the other one. I bet you could stand over there and you don't see it because it's too fast. But I see it. Sometime they hit it in the vein, right? Hit it, and he pull out right away. I know in a minute, the blood start come out. Not right away. I know this rooster can [not go far]. Because when the blood start coming out they grow weak. The blood come from his mouth, from the vein, from his nose. And we know, it's very dangerous, when the rooster wounded. That's when we bet, 500 to 300, 5 to 2. You have to be very, very smart, if you like to be at cockfight. But we all friends, like family. Never you see a fight inside, two men. We drink beer, whiskey. But the rooster fight, not the men.

Collected by Geoffrey Biddle, "Alphabet City," Lower East Side, 1978 [11]

buildings, the closest that most will come to controlling property, however tenuously." [12]

In her work on leisure on the Lower East Side of New York, Suzanne Wasserman writes about the cellar clubs, which sprang up in the 1930s. [13] They were an indigenous response by young people to their unemployment on the one hand and to the adult-run settlement houses on the other. The clubs offered what the settlement houses could not provide—privacy and a welcome lack of supervision.

The Fralou Social Club, like many of the others, grew out of the conditions of the Depression. "We were all broke. Not one of us had a job. For half a year all we had for clubrooms was the steps of a boarded-up house." [14] The group finally did achieve a clubhouse; but just as readily as meeting places were established, they were lost. When the Wa-Cor Social Club lost their basement, they had to start meeting on the stoop above their former cellar club. The clubs were only a step away from the stoop. Young people struggled for their own spaces to play, for the space they needed for teenage forms of play—gambling, "hanging out," and "making out," activities not well suited to the street and the front stoop. For these, they sought out the basements and cellars of the urban landscape.

Opposite: Cockfight, Lower East Side, Manhattan, 1978 (Photo by Geoffrey Biddle, "Alphabet City")

Since [the lot] has a Puerto Rican–style house and garden and a laterine like in Puerto Rico, it seems like Puerto Rico—because in no other place [in New York] are you going to feel like you're in Puerto Rico. Here you see tomatoes, peppers, eggplants. . . . Look, the bottom part of the house is made from bamboo, and where you find bamboo is in Puerto Rico. And here everybody likes to whistle in the style of the *coquí* [a variety of frog found in Puerto Rico], which is something typically Puerto Rican, because there is nothing more Puerto Rican than the *coquí.*

José Manuel "Chema" Soto, born 1947, member of the Rincon Criollo casita, South Bronx [15]

CONTROL

Unsanctioned activities play a part in urban life, and it is often the underside of the urban landscape which affords the privacy for that side of life—under the boardwalk, beneath the highway, in the cellar. Sex, and illegal activities, such as cockfighting and playing the numbers, require privacy and secrecy. A New Yorker lost his virginity in a rooftop pigeon coop.[16] Another woman said that her grandfather, born on the Lower East Side in the 1880s, fondly recalled another rooftop operator in his neighborhood, nicknamed "Penny Hump." Ellen Summers, who grew up on Coney Island, said that the boardwalk was an ideal surface for skipping, but that under the boardwalk "was where there was smoking and drinking and making out—that was where I wasn't allowed."[17] Comedian David Brenner claims his childhood friends referred to this location as "Hotel Underwood."

I used to live next to the St. Moritz in the building called Number 40 on Central Park South—and we lived on the second to the top floor, and on the top floor there was an elevator shaft—the top of it was closed off and plastered over and painted and it created an area that if you traveled up a 45-degree angle you'd come to a flat place on the top. It was dark, hidden, and inaccessible—it was perfect!

So what we would do is—you could get up there—on one side there was no wall at first so it required somebody kind of nimble to scrabble up the first part, but once you got up a quarter of the way you could get your hands on the two walls of the corridor and force your way up to the top—it helped if you had shoes that didn't have leather soles, or bare feet. A lot of bare feet. And the real trick for getting up there with comics in your hands, or flashlights, chewing bubble gum was to find a way to hang the stuff on your body so that you could get up—'cause there was no way to hold on to anything if you were to make it to the top. But the reward for getting to the top was that you and your friend could have this secret spot that belonged to you rent-free—a perfect little clubhouse.

Interviewer: And a rent-free place on 40 Central Park South is very valuable.

And let me add that coming down when you left was the real treat. 'Cause then you didn't have to scrabble up, all you had to do was sit down and shoot down the slide.

Susan Mildred Brown, 1940s and '50s, Central Park South, Manhattan

---

Battling for Turf

On a street or city block, children, the elderly, automobile drivers, parents, store owners, strangers, the fire department, sanitation workers, and city authorities must negotiate the use of space. Sometimes children battle over whose metaphor will prevail. An argument will break out over whether a particular fence is the hull of a ship for one group's fantasy or a "jail" for another's game of tag. Other times, battles are fought between

I remember an old man in my neighborhood in Brooklyn named Jack Fraca. He lives on an apartment house on Sixth Avenue and Garfield Place a block away from me. He told me that across the street from him there was an open lot, and one night when he was a little boy he looked out the window and saw Al Capone duking it out with another guy for local supremacy while a bunch of local thugs stood around and watched. He also told me that after Al Capone made it big in Chicago, he would drive by in a big car and throw $100 bills out the window to repay the old neighborhood.

Glen Abel, born 1948,
Park Slope, Brooklyn

Savage Nomads gang jacket, the Bronx,
1970s (Photo by Richard Lawrence Stack,
courtesy of Access Bronx)

CONTROL

children and the elderly; older adults may not believe in the "right to free play," and children may not respect the needs of the elderly for peace and quiet.

The young also compete with one another for public space. Sometimes the battles are mild, nonviolent. As Peter Melia described his neighborhood block warfare in the 1930s, "we're going to walk on your block if you walk on mine."[18] But frequently turf struggles erupt into fistfights and "rumbles." Writing about the period from 1900 to 1920, David Nasaw notes:

> The cities were divided by block and gang. Gang fighting to protect turf or extend it into the vacant lot next door was commonplace and often ferocious. Kids fought with paving stones, bottles, bricks, and garbage can lids as shields until one side, bloodied and bowed, was forced to retreat. The wars appeared to outsiders to be ethnically inspired, especially when the combatants called each other Sheeny, Christ-killer, Dago and Mickie. But it was space, not ethnicity or religion they fought over. Territory was everything to the children. It was, indeed, the only thing they could call their own.[19]

Oftentimes, gang warfare and gang subcultures grow out of play peer groups. In a study of delinquent subcultures conducted in the 1950s, Lloyd E. Ohlin reports many gang members tracing the origin of their gangs to stickball clubs. "Indio said it [the club] started in 1947. The Regals were a stickball team. Since they were a Puerto Rican group, they resented other groups, mainly Negro, who were coming over from ———, the western part of the neighborhood, to date their girls."[20]

Playing the numbers is part of the tapestry of the Black community. In Brownsville, when I was growing up around 1965, there was a candy store on the corner of Saratoga and Livonia. It was so cool you could send your kid to the store with your bet.

Izzy's poolroom was another place. The heavier bettors came to the poolroom. Two white guys owned it, but they allowed the numbers writers to hang out there. I was tall so I was able to get in the poolroom, and I learned to shoot real well. When my mother died, things got kind of heavy, and they sort of took me in. I got a job there cleaning up. My job was to "steer." I would steer people to the numbers writers—the bookies—because a lot of times they would change for whatever reason—someone got into a fight or got locked up. And I would also screen the customers. I'd say "I know his father, I know his mother—I know he's not the police."

During the holidays, the numbers men would come around and give people in the neighborhood turkeys and give their children toys. So the people would protect them. When the cops came around, they would protect them because they didn't want anybody coming around and taking their turkey man.

Sam Lee, born 1950, Brownsville, Brooklyn

The Cadets, Lower East Side, Manhattan, 1978 (Photo © Martha Cooper/ City Lore)

The history of street battles from the 1880s to the present reveals a vast escalation in weaponry. Henry Noble MacCracken recalls how his 1880s gang fought "The Great Whip War" with the "Micks," escalating the level of violence by introducing the riding whip, a common piece of paraphernalia in a horse-drawn city.[21] In the 1950s, gangs fought with zip guns and switchblades, and deaths became commonplace; but these battles seem tame when contrasted with today's drug wars fought not over control over play spaces, but over business rights to drug turf—and fought not with fists and knives but with automatic weapons.

The East Side, for children, was a world plunged in eternal war. It was suicide to walk into the next block. Each block was a separate nation, and when a strange boy appeared, the patriots swarmed.

"What streeter?" was demanded, furiously.

"Chrystie Street," was the trembling reply.

BANG! This was the signal for a mass assault on the unlucky foreigner, with sticks, stones, fists, and feet. The beating was as cruel and bloody as that of grown-ups; no mercy was shown. I have had three holes in my head, and many black eyes and puffed lips from our street wars. We did it to others, they did it to us. It was patriotism, though what difference there was between one East Side block and another is now hard to see.

Michael Gold, born 1894, Lower East Side[22]

CONTROL

Growing up in the city around 1935 to 1940 had many hazards to it. A Jewish kid walking out of the neighborhood of Brownsville walking north would be assaulted by Italian kids—if one went northeast the Polish kids would get us, and northeast by northeast the Lithuanians would—south were again Italians and southwest were the Irish—so getting out of our neighborhood involved some complex maneuvers. However, there were many contradictions in this. The block I lived in was virtually all Jewish but there were a couple of Italian families. And I can still remember vividly the day that Tony Mazzoli came running down the street alerting everybody "The wops are coming, the wops are coming!" He identified more with his own street than with his own ethnic compatriots—and that was the pattern of street life at that period of time.

Lou Singer, born 1925, Brownsville, Brooklyn

We always counted stoops because the sense of family and friendship was according to the block. And kids would say, "I'll meet you on the fourth stoop." You would know all this information about how many stoops there were on your block and how many windows in your building; that was really important. The block was also identified: that was the Irish block, and that was the Italian block. On our block it was Jews and Puerto Ricans. Everyone sort of had their little turf divided up. It was even more pronounced for gang members later. But for us, it started that way: you were from this block. Later with gangs, it was sometimes several blocks. The bigger the gangs, the more blocks, the more turf they had. The Latin Gents had eight blocks. By the time I got to high school, they moved all the way up to my junior high school, which was pretty far; it's over a mile. They started out with eight blocks, then they got bigger and bigger.

Isabel Alvarez, born 1950, the Bronx

In the 1970s, there were seventy-six gangs in the South Bronx—the Ghetto Brothers, the Savage Nomads, the Black Spades, Savage Skulls, the Golden Guineas, and many others. It was a subculture that lasted ten years. And gang jackets were very important. . . . They're a work of art . . . sort of an identity. They thought of it as "the second me." . . . Some of the gang members were buried with the jackets and usually if you left the gang, the gang jacket was burned. . . .

And in those days, every three blocks you would be on different turf and you had to respect that. You didn't fly your colors when you walked through other turf, you wore your jacket inside out. Now if I'm going to a certain neighborhood that belongs to a certain gang, let's say for example the Savage Nomads and I'm a Ghetto Brother, I would have to turn the jacket inside out to show respect—that I'm entering the area to visit a relative or a friend. . . . When you would rumble with another gang, then you turned your jackets around and flew your colors.

Carmello Diaz, born 1957, the South Bronx

Struggling with the Automobile

Street sprinkler wagon (Drawing by Paul Frenzeny, Harper's Weekly, *3 August 1872; photo © Martha Cooper/City Lore)*

"A whole, lost, urban folklore grew up among the children of the 19th-century horse-propelled city."

COLIN WARD, *A CHILD IN THE CITY*[23]

The horse-drawn city moved at a much slower pace. Vehicles traveled more slowly. Children could easily hitch rides on the backs of carts. Eighty-two-year-old Sofie Degner recalls that the more daring boys would hitch their sleds to a horse-drawn wagon.[24] Livestock were a source of amusement. Gene Schermerhorn lassoed pigs along Sixth Avenue, and children wove braided rings and bracelets out of horses' tails. And they shaped rings out of horseshoe nails found in the gutters, sometimes flattening them on the trolley tracks.[25] Michael Gold writes about

CONTROL

Sledding at 51st Street and Fifth Avenue, Brooklyn, 1924 (Municipal Archives of the City of New York)

[When we were growing up at the turn of the century], ice wagons had a convenient step at the back of them upon which we used to "hitch," stealing a piece of ice upon which to suck or being content to stand on the step and to watch the asphalt fly beneath our feet as the big brown horses pulled the yellow ice-wagon fast along the streets.

Ethel and Oliver Hale, born 1891, 1893, Harlem, Manhattan[28]

dead horses on New York streets at the turn of the century, "another plaything in the queer and terrible treasury of East Side childhood."[26]

The coming of the automobile created a life-and-death struggle over public space. In her book, *Pricing the Priceless Child,* Viviana Zelizer traces the way in which the automobile gradually pushed the children back from the streets—accident by accident, each one resulting in an outcry of protest against the drivers, but each inexorably changing the nature of play.[27] In 1922, 15,000 New York City children paraded up Fifth Avenue to a Child Memorial to accident victims. They were followed by fifty "White Star Mothers" who had lost their children to the deadly automobile. In 1922, 477 children were killed by cars in New York City. In 1988, the number was down to 46, suggesting that fewer children are playing in the streets (and a tribute to improved medical care). May Day, 1926, was a nationally declared "No Accident Day." A crowd stood silently at the unveiling of two memorials in memory of the boys and girls killed in traffic accidents in the previous year.

Where the Eddie Grant Parkway is, or whatever they call it, was known as Busco Milan Hill, and the 167th cross-town line went up there, from Jerome Avenue it went all the way up to University Avenue, six, seven, eight blocks, and there was quite a hill, not a precipitous hill, but a very good hill. So we would take our sleds up to University Avenue, put one runner in the track, once the trolley car came through, because we knew there wouldn't be another one for about twelve to fifteen minutes, we would put one runner into the track, the other runner of course was outside the track, and we'd just sit down there and it steered itself. All the way down. . . . I'm talking up till 1917, 1918, after that the Concourse began to get a little more crowded. The Model Ts were out, the big Pierce Arrows for those who could afford it. So there was no more sleigh riding.

Samuel A. Feuchtwanger, born 1905, the Bronx

Child hitching a ride, Lower East Side, Manhattan, 1978 (Photo © Martha Cooper/City Lore)

CONTROL

Anyone who grew up in the South Bronx when I did would know what 'hindu' meant—if a play was interrupted by a car or some other obstacle, someone would say, "That's a hindu, do it again." If the player had made a successful play before the interference and made another successful play when he did it over, he would say, "Cheeky, Chose, Always Goes. . . ." If you don't know these things you weren't from New York in the '30s and '40s.

John McGrath, born 1930, the Bronx

Boy flying a kite, Lower East Side, Manhattan (Photo by Bruce Davidson, Magnum Photos, Inc.)

CITY PLAY

All the horses that stopped in the block were our source of supply. But Ole Sole's horse was the one we patronized most. We could pull only one hair at a time. It came out easily. The horse just turned around and looked kind of reproachfully. But when we tried to pull more than one, he flinched and kicked and the hair did not come out.

We got old wooden spools and hammered four nails in the top. On these we placed four strings of horsehair, and braided them by pulling them through the spool. It made a dandy watch fob.

Jimmy Savo, born 1895, the Bronx[29]

But the adult world was not crying out against the automobile, and the restrictions they sought were not on cars but on children. Motorized vehicles redefined the use of streets and changed notions of public space. Adults used city ordinances to make street play illegal, and they used the playground movement and other reform efforts to coax children, especially poor immigrants, from the sidewalks. The children were losing the battle for the streets. In 1921, one fourteen-year-old boy observed, "a child doesn't make traffic rules, drive cars, etc. The child's main object is to keep out of the way of moving vehicles."[30]

Cars and buses, trolleys and subways replaced horses and wooden carriages as moving surfaces of the city. They increased the mobility of the adult world, but constricted the child's. They altered the feel of the city for children and other players, forcing them to move out of the way, tying up curb space, and giving the city a faster pace and a new texture of metal and steel.

The car was an agent of change. It was part of an inevitable movement to control childhood, to domesticate it—to keep it off the streets. These large, looming contraptions drove surprised children from the streets and put public space more firmly in the hands of adults. Children fought back by incorporating cars into their games and continuing to play amid traffic, but eventually they lost. As Abe Lass put it, the central difference between children's play in the early twentieth century and today is that "children no longer own the streets."[31]

Reforming Play

"The children . . . dramatized their conception of the famous Society for the Prevention of Cruelty to Children [by imagining it] as an ogre that would catch them."

LILLIAN WALD, *THE HOUSE ON HENRY STREET*[32]

Beginning in the middle to the late nineteenth century, a number of reformers attempted to mold children's play, and in particular the play of poor immigrant children. They saw in organized play and sport ways to ameliorate social ills associated with the effects of new immigration (which crowded New York's streets with chil-

Note the child carefully following directions on the sign. Central Park, 1969 (Photo © Nancy Rudolph)

dren), and industrialization (which provided not only cheap commercial entertainments such as amusement parks, dance halls, and professional sports, but also the forms of transportation to get there).[33] One of the reformers' strategies was to take children off the street and supervise their play in controlled spaces, including parks, playgrounds, and designated "play streets."

The vast effort to domesticate play, this adult "conspiracy" to keep play off the streets, to smooth its ragged edges, begins with the imposition of mandatory public schooling in 1842; it continues with park movement (plans for Central Park were drawn up in 1853); and the Fresh Air Fund, founded in 1877, which plucked youngsters out of their deprived urban environment for summer vacations in the country. This movement, sometimes called "child saving," established settlement houses such as Hull-House in Chicago (1889), and Henry Street (1894) and the Christodora House (1897) on the Lower East Side of New York.

In 1902, New York's Board of Estimate appropriated money for the equipment and maintenance of Seward Park, the first municipal playground in New York City. The Playground Association of America was founded in 1906 by Henry Curtis, and by 1910 thousands of city playgrounds provided organized play activities for urban children. Curtis developed a model playground curriculum that "play directors" supervising the playgrounds were encouraged to follow:

1:30–2:00, patriotic songs
2:00–2:30, supervised "free play": tugs-of-war, marbles, etc.
2:30–3:30, track and field events
3:30–5:00, team games, vocational training, and folk dancing[34]

The Police Athletic League was founded in 1914, and Police Commissioner Arthur Woods asked police captains in the city to seek out vacant lots that could be used for play spaces.[35] By the mid-1920s, the "play street" movement, which closes off city streets for children, was in full force (it continues to this day). "Children born between 1880 and 1920," writes Bernard Mergen, "played under the watchful eyes of the first generation of psy-

---

I had just finished a bicycle education training program . . . but I realized that the girls can't really relate to cycling in a competitive form. The boys were coming out. But I knew we had to do something for the girls. So I kept waiting and waiting and got a call one day. Someone wanted to use Central Park as a discothèque, and as part of the discothèque they wanted to do some double dutch for the mothers. And when I heard the expression double dutch about a thousand bulbs lit in my mind. I started realizing it was an activity that girls really related to. . . . Mothers did it when they were kids. . . . See the relationship—mother—clothesline—daughter. . . .

And in order to make a program you have to sell it to the parents, and if you deal with mothers of disadvantaged children or disadvantaged mothers . . . it's got to be something they can be happy with. So I did some research and talked to about twenty parents, asked them whether or not they would go for this program and the two things that came out of the discussion were, yes, we like it, we can talk to our kids about it. [But] we're tired of these programs that are not organized. I [told them] they're organized, there's going to be some form of control in a respectful way. . . .

I've been criticized by some folks . . . how can I take a play activity and convert it into a competition. Most play activities were converted into competition in the world today—boxing, baseball, and any other sport that's competitive in nature, can be played recreationally or competitively; that's what the world is about.

David Walker, president of the Double Dutch League, New York[36]

CONTROL

A "Post No Bills" sign becomes a basket, Brooklyn, 1950s (Photo by Arthur Leipzig)

chologists, playground supervisors, and parents who had been made anxious by the need to maintain traditional standards in the face of rapid change." [37]

This movement to reform play, with its complex motivations and amorphous results, is one of the most intriguing subjects in the history of American ideas (see Afterword). From its inception in the nineteenth century to the present, the effort to organize free constructive play activities for poor children, and profit-based activities for wealthier children, continues unabated with Little League, scouting, and a wide variety of lessons, along with commercial magazines and videos which offer "parenting ideas" for organizing and fostering children's play.

Go-cart made from a police barricade, Lower Manhattan, 1978 (Photo © Martha Cooper/City Lore)

CONTROL

Street double dutch, West 115th Street, Manhattan, 1968 (Photo © Katrina Thomas)

From an adult perspective, children's play is a resource: toy companies see it as a market for their products, and community leaders see it as a way of shaping good citizens. In 1973, the Police Athletic League began to see the potential in double dutch and helped organize the Double Dutch Tournament. Barbara Kirshenblatt-Gimblett quotes Detective Williams's lament in 1980 that there was no obvious product associated with jumping rope which would serve as an incentive for corporate interest: "You can't patent a jump rope. All you have to do is take down a clothesline, use it, and put it back up. There's no product like a hula hoop or a Frisbee."[38]

Nonetheless, two years later McDonald's Restaurants became an official sponsor of the sport, and the tournament grew in size and scope. Held in the plaza at Lincoln Center outside the Metropolitan Opera, the announcers and organizers refer to double dutch as "street ballet."[39]

In fact, this new sport may be as close to ballet than it is to street double dutch. "Competition," writes Barbara Kirshenblatt-Gimblett, "intensifies both regimentation and innovation. For scoring purposes, the activity is highly formalized and moves are standardized. In the case of double dutch, regular practice ensures that the required movements are executed precisely according to the rule book. However, the free-style category institutionalizes innovation. The inventiveness exhibited in double dutch goes beyond anything generally seen on the street."[40] Participation in the contests is often linked to good school grades and scholarships.

Since the beginning of the nineteenth century, folklorists have been a voice advocating for free play in the wake of the reformers (see Afterword). When the double dutch league was being formed in the 1970s, Herbert and Mary Knapp, two collectors of children's games, worried: "[The tournament] would reduce the

Rule 14
Turners may hold the knot handle of the official rope with the knot facing downward, upward or with the knot held in the palm of the hand. When holding the knot in the palm of the hand, the finger of the hand must be between the double ropes.
Rule 15
Turner may not turn double handed during any of the scored events.

Double dutch rule book, 1979 (Photo © Martha Cooper/City Lore)

CONTROL

complex verbal, physical, and social interplay of traditional jump-rope to mere jumping. Worse, when adults take over, they immediately announce, 'There's a right way and wrong way,' and begin demanding that children play 'right.' We know a boy who grew to hate going to school while his gym teacher was 'teaching' jump-rope. She said he was 'galloping' instead of 'jumping.' He was convinced that he couldn't even pass playtime."[41]

In today's New York, double dutch—and other autonomous and sometimes rebellious street forms—are co-opted to suit adult purposes; graffiti artists are invited to paint wall murals for the city, and social agencies sponsor breakdancing competitions, with greater or lesser success. The reformers are sometimes up against subcultures whose activities are difficult to redirect precisely because the defining element is not the expression of art or play but the opposition to authority groups.

At the same time as adults try to co-opt the play activities of children, children often subvert adult efforts to regulate their play. In the Marcy Projects in Bedford-Stuyvesant, Brooklyn, in the sixties, hitting the "No Ball Playing" sign earned the player an extra score in the game of points;[42] on the Lower East Side in the 1980s, children built a go-cart out of a police barricade. Playgrounds designed for children are used in unintended ways; they climb up the sliding board and, using cardboard, slide down the jungle gym. Children and adults engage in an endless struggle to remake the world in their own image—adults organizing the play activities of children, and children incorporating these adult efforts into their improvised and spontaneous play world.

I grew up with many boys and girls my age who lived in the New York City Housing Authority–sponsored projects that were newly opened at the time. . . . So I traveled in groups of children numbering as large as twenty-five to thirty-five kids. This allowed me the most wonderful opportunity to participate in large organized group games. It also meant I had loads of friends to visit.

My parents worked until 5:00 so I had an after-school snack club who visited the apartment I lived in to drink chocolate milk and eat toasted Wonder bread with butter and watch television cartoon shows. When I was old enough to join the after-school center at the Patrick Henry School, I participated in woodworking shops led by Mr. Kessler. When I was fourteen my mother allowed me to join the evening community center at J.H.S. 13 where I played pool, ping pong, chess, checkers, and basketball with my brothers and friends—Irving, Chino, Fredo, Justo, Michael, Kirwin, Jeddy, Papo, Laddy, Jujo, Johny Co-Co-Lo, Calvin, Eggie, Moses, Billy, Icy, Benny, and David, along with Candela and Canapa Head. The most amazing thing was when George Penon hit the longest soaring home run I ever seen in the schoolyard against his cousins—Screwhead and Odd-Job—to the grass field against 60 East 106th St.

George Hernandez, born 1958, East Harlem, Manhattan

Steven Zeitlin

CHAPTER

FIVE

CONCLUSION:
A
COMMUNITY
ROOTED
IN
PLACE

Previous page: Bedspring becomes a trampoline, Bedford-Stuyvesant, Brooklyn, 1985 (Photo by Steven Zeitlin, Queens Council on the Arts)

Steven Saraband spent his childhood playing stickball in the Bronx. His block "dead ended" onto a street lined with apartment buildings, so when the ball was hit long, there was always the possibility that it would travel at an angle into that blind spot where the batter could not see the results of the play. Twenty years ago, the score stood 3 to 2 with a player on base in the last inning of a crucial neighborhood stickball game. Saraband's teammate hit a long fly ball deep into the blind spot. The team began cheering the game-winning home run, when suddenly around the corner the outfielder appears. "I caught the ball—you're out," he cried. There was nothing to do but fight, and they did—the biggest fistfight of the year.

Girls performing "cheers" at the Marcy Projects, Bedford-Stuyvesant, Brooklyn, 1985 (Photo by Steven Zeitlin, Queens Council on the Arts)

CITY PLAY

Twenty years later Steve Saraband organized a reunion of his friends from that block in the Bronx. The purpose was to return to the street and play the current residents, a group of Puerto Rican and Black teenagers, at the tenacious street games which had taken root on that block, transcending ethnicity and generations (Saraband, a filmmaker, was planning to film the event). When the two stickball players who had started the fight all those years ago met, one asked the other, "You know, after all these years I still have one question . . ."

Before he could finish, his friend replied, "I did catch that ball."[1]

This episode and the other reminiscences in this book testify to the "durable character of childhood" which, as Gaston Bachelard has written, "returns to animate broad sections of adult life."[2] It also suggests the way certain places preserve a fragile ecology which nurtures traditional games. A generation later, when an entirely new collection of children animated that block, many of the same childhood games still flourished on that particular configuration of streets in the Bronx.

Street games require a special habitat. They need a sufficient number of children to make the games possible—some games require three or four people on each team; they necessitate a particular spatial configuration so that the games can be played without too many interruptions of traffic; they need a sufficient level of safety for parents to permit a measure of freedom for children on the street; and they require a neighborhood lifestyle that holds "stoop life" in high esteem, that regards twilights on the amphitheater of the stoop, watching the comings and goings of people, or playing until the ball is lost in the darkness, more exciting than an evening of television.

The street that lives, writes Charles J. Zerner,

> is a street whose buildings are no more than three stories high, permitting visual, acoustical, and immediate physical access to the life below. . . . [It] is one that has . . . a living, vital topography of dwellings . . . with porches, thresholds, platforms on which children can gather. These foster activities that need a certain remove from the street, yet intimate connection with it. These stairways and porches, thresholds and landings, shelter young children playing with dolls, setting up miniature shops, playing chess and checkers, doing their homework, and having intimate conversations. They are places to rest, to observe the spectacle upon the street, and be physically linked and in touch with the home. It is here, on steps and stoops, the very lowest in a series of vertical thresholds, that we frequently find the youngest of all children playing.[3]

In the 1930s and '40s, Oscar and Ethel Hale compiled a thousand-page single-spaced manuscript called "From Sidewalk, Gutter, and Stoop," about traditional games on the streets of New York. They documented hundreds of different games and hun-

Breakdancing, Jamaica, Queens, 1984 (Photo © Martha Cooper/City Lore)

dreds of variations of each of those games. They included not only "Double Dutch," but also "Double Irish," "Double Dodge," "French Fried," "French Dutch," and "Double Jewish."[4]

Half a century later, we did not find anywhere near the number or variety of games played out of doors. In the 1980s, far fewer blocks preserve that confluence of lifestyle and urban geography that sustain the traditional games and outdoor play. The photographs of Martha Cooper taken on the Lower East Side in the seventies reveal a life very different from the Leipzig photos from the forties, where Red Rover, ring-a-leavio, and Johnny on the pony were played by large groups of children on the sidewalks and street. In her photographs, we do not see large groups of children choosing up sides and organizing traditional games. Cooper's pictures have one, two, sometimes three children on their own in empty lots or broken sidewalks.

In the poorer neighborhoods which Cooper visited in Harlem and the Lower East Side, we still do find children playing outdoors, creatively manipulating their environment. In these neighborhoods, interiors are smaller, less comfortable, often un-airconditioned, and the street offers open space and fresh air. In some neighborhoods such as Bedford-Stuyvesant's Marcy Projects, half a dozen ropes still turn on a hot day. Groups of five or six girls perform "cheers," a chanted, dance ensemble piece with hand-clapping and improvised (often obscene) verses. Groups of girls rehearse in private so that rival groups will not "steal" their cheers; and sometimes they try out their chants on the roaring subways where they can sing at the top of their lungs and hardly disturb their fellow riders.

The changes in city play over the past one hundred years are tied to the changes in city life over the past few generations. In his book *A History of Children's Play,* Brian Sutton-Smith offers an extraordinary analysis of some of the complex changes affecting play. Partly because of what he regards as his own optimistic outlook, this New Zealand–born scholar sees many of the changes in play for the better. He suggests that the contemporary forms of play with electronic toys and television are less physically violent than the earlier outdoor games; although the fantasies on television and in video games are all about war, children are not actually bullying each other on the playground.

These electronic diversions and creative playthings, he suggests, also provide the kind of training our children need for the world which they will inherit. The manual world of the nineteenth century has been replaced by a world of signs and symbols, in which information systems and particularly television play a major role. "It is now necessary," he writes, "to produce generations of children who can be innovative, not in killing birds with catapults but in ideas for use in mass media, advertising, selling, bureaucratizing, computing, education, and so on."[5]

Today, when children gather after school and face the recurrent question of what to do, street games are only one possibility, which must compete with a wide range of organized sports and commercial amusements along with television and radio.

> When life is full of . . . an ever-changing round of "fads and fancies," ranging from a new record album which one "simply must have," to the reincarnation of Batman at the local movie theater . . . unrewarded perseverance at the old traditional games may seem pointless. . . . Sports and modern entertainment bring in their train adult interest and encouragement. Traditional games whose only incentive is the enjoyment of playing them cannot compete with these other influences. That any such games still persist is testament to the intrinsic importance and meaningfulness of those games to the players.[6]

CONCLUSION

You can take the kid out of New York City but you can't take New York City out of the kid, according to an enthusiastic group of expatriates living here. That is the spirit behind the New York City Street Games Fair in San Francisco, held today for the 7th time. Despite overcast skies and a chill wind, about 1,500 former New Yorkers and their families gathered to play stickball, punchball, double dutch jump rope, stoopball and other games of their youth.

New York Times,
September 30, 1985[7]

Many of the new games that have flourished on the streets of New York bear this out; some, like double dutch, thrive partly in competitive, adult-run forums such as the annual double dutch competition at Lincoln Center; even the ghetto-fostered style of gymnastics performed on discarded mattresses and box springs has become a formal adult-sponsored performance with groups such as the Flip Boys. Other activities, deliberately antagonistic to public, polite adult society, thrive on the streets but have as their purpose engaging the interest and attention—and sometimes the rage—of the adult world. Graffiti, which may appear to be a kind of random vandalism to the uninitiated, is, from the perspective of the writers, a game played for the "fame" which comes from having one's code name read all over the city by one's peers. Breakdancing, while it has some roots in mock fighting, is largely a performance genre, played for recognition, for prizes, for prestige, for the money which can come from street performance, and for a ticket out of the ghetto; it is a long way from marbles or skelly played to while away an afternoon. Similarly, rapping, a street tradition of competitive verbal artistry fostered at block and playground parties in Black neighborhoods, is now intimately tied to the recording industry that promotes and markets the music.

Adult controls and the electronic media have affected the freedom and inclination of the young to move freely across the gameboard of the city's streets. But the gameboard itself has changed. In the course of a hundred years, the surface of the city changed as streets were paved, as vacant lots were filled, as buildings grew taller and playgrounds were constructed. The human element has also changed, as waves of immigrants who flowed into New York with the shifts in laws in the 1840s, 1880s, and again in the 1960s, created new patterns of residence.

As the dangers of city living—fears of kidnapping, crime, and drugs—became more marked through the years, middle-class parents have tended to keep their children inside, or send them to camp, rather than allow them to play unsupervised on the streets. "Modern children," writes Brian Sutton-Smith, "spend an increasingly large part of their lives by themselves with their toys, a situation inconceivable several centuries ago. The video game is the apotheosis of this trend."[8]

Television and commercialized toys also encourage indoor play; but beyond the hours which are spent in front of the screen instead of on the street, the media also affects the relationship of the player to the urban environment. With television, people don't necessarily live where they are.[9] They are "tuned into" a world very different from the block.

Generations of New York City children have adapted their play activities to changes in the urban landscape, adjusting their games to the increasing density and verticality of the city. Despite the encroachment of tall buildings, vehicular traffic, and adults into children's play spaces, traditional games and improvised play have survived outdoors. But the incursions of television and electronic diversions on the one hand and crime and drugs on the other present obstacles of a new magnitude.

Today, mass culture has become part of the urban environment, and some city residents incorporate it into their play activities. Barbara Kirshenblatt-Gimblett describes how

> people transform, parody, subvert, and otherwise actively rework and renew what is offered by mass production. . . . They also look to the popularization of urban vernacular forms [such as breakdancing and rap music] as a source of political power. . . Most recently voguing, a [dance form associated with drag balls which mimics poses from *Vogue* magazine] . . . has been reappropriated by the very fashion industry it parodies and can be seen on more mainstream dance floors. Breaking, rapping, and now voguing . . . reveal the ingenuity of city people in reworking mass culture for their own purposes.[10]

Rap music, breakdancing, and hip-hop culture in the Black and Puerto Rican communities attest to the vitality of street tradition and the way it responds to new urban needs. While television draws people away from the street, radio and cassette tapes, a key element in breaking and rap music, are played on boom boxes or "ghetto blasters" and are integral to the culture of many streets.

Certainly, the creative spirit does not shrivel up and die in the wake of mass media; but for many of the city kids whom the media catapults into the limelight, short-lived fame has disastrous effects. Henry Chalfant, who worked with some of the early breakdancing crews when they became successful, tells about seeing one of the former crew members recently in Washington Heights. "He is a bright man, lucid about his situation, and he said, 'Look at me, I'm eighteen years old and my life is over. I've done everything. I've traveled to Europe, I even shook hands with the Queen of England and now I'm selling crack on the street.'"[11]

But beyond its effect on individuals who are swept up in the whirlwind of fame (which can be positive as well as negative), the media has a deleterious effect on communities. The reminiscences of New Yorkers recorded for City Play reveal something more than a nostalgia for childhood games and the places where they were played; they disclose a sensitivity to the communities that had their roots on the block, the kinds of communities that are threatened by the media and by the increasing dangers of city life.

To certain extent, Sutton-Smith is correct in his optimism. Children's games and toys, though store-bought, are often very creative, and certainly they are well suited to our times; the same is true with many television programs. But while bought toys, television, and video games may encourage certain kinds of individual play, they don't create communities. They are placeless; the world they create is on the screen—in the mind—not on the block.

CONCLUSION

All play was suspended when certain radio programs were on. *Uncle Don* who would tell you on your birthday where your present was hidden (I actually heard the program that got him fired from the air). *The Green Hornet, The Shadow,* and the program with the squeaking door—can't remember the name. This one you had to listen with the lights off—real scary.
*Francine Kern, born 1932,
Richmond Hill, Queens*

I was six years old in 1974. We used to play a game called TV tag. When the person who was it made a lunge for you, you'd call out the name of a TV show. You'd yell out "All in the Family"—it was a test of your TV knowledge because you couldn't repeat a show. You would run out of shows eventually.

Robin Eisgrau, born 1968,
Flushing, Queens

The media can't replace the real experiences of growing up and getting to know a city street; it can't create a sense of place. Even drugs, which have ravaged urban communities in ways far more destructive than television, are a way out of neighborhoods and locales; in the television-soaked America of today, young people become frustrated with communities and relationships which have none of the glamour of the world depicted on television; advertisements remind them constantly of what they do not have. Ironically, the fear of drugs and crime keeps city residents locked in their apartments, allowing nothing in except television and feeding the vicious cycle. Local communities have been devalued in contemporary American life, which emphasizes success stories and celebrities in the constant barrage of the media.

Children whose lives really turn on the block draw the most minute distinctions in their environment; Hamilton Fish Armstrong writes about roller skating down his Sixth Avenue block and knowing who lived in each house without looking up—he could tell by the particular buzz created by the pavement on his feet;[12] other children distinguished between "kite hill" and "vulture's hill" and "dead man's curve," and knew such exotic places such as the Casbah—which was a nickname for the railing (the "cäz-bar") leading up to the entrance of P.S. 1 in Long Island City, Queens.[13] The block was a place to be from.

The children who play on the streets of New York not only play together, they often see each other every day in many contexts. They learn how to share spaces together, and build relationships and bonds with the neighborhood. Their communities do not revolve around a single interest such as Little League or bingo. When social interactions move beyond a single interest, and people become involved in a multiplicity of ways, communities are born; relationships move beyond a simple use and exchange, and take on new meaning. As one New York taxi driver put it, a real neighborhood is where the butcher comes to your funeral.

"I don't want a Childhood City," writes Colin Ward. "I want a city where children live in the same world as I do."[14] Folklorists often speak of children's games and rhymes as part of the "secret society of children," but the traditional games are only one component of a lifestyle which includes both adults and children who are involved on a day-to-day basis on a patch of urban turf they come to think of as their own.

Erving Goffman writes about the invisible membrane that forms around players intent upon their game. But there is another kind of membrane that pulls across the block, that contains the varied groups of children, the different ages at their play. It is a membrane created by the adults, a safety net, a web of sociability and unobtrusive vigilance that enables children to create secret societies and play worlds that swell and burst out of harm's way.

"The street that lets children dwell," writes Charles J. Zerner, "also allows the dwelling of the generations on their journey through time. These were not places that were designated or bounded for the dwelling of children alone. A simple stair, a porch, a threshold in the sun, wide enough to sit upon, a street, quiet enough will let appear the dwelling of parents, grandparents,

Dancing girls, Yorkville, Manhattan, 1962 (Photo by Builder Levy)

CONCLUSION

Many years later I went back to the old neighborhood. I was taking a friend there. And I was looking around and walking down the old streets seeing the new residents just going about their business there. I got the feeling that they don't know the place the way I did. I know the secrets of this place. I know its past. And there's a frustration about people's ignorance for not knowing that. It's just a building to them, and it might just as well have always been what it is now.

Don Fellman, born 1949,
Long Island City, Queens

cousins and neighbors, children and infants."[15] Traditional games and play come from a community that is comfortable enough with itself to sustain play worlds within the other, more problematic real worlds it must live in and face.

The true measure of this city of New York—and other cities—is the degree to which it can nurture and protect this core activity. Many New Yorkers who live in high-rise housing projects, for instance, complain about the deleterious effect of their living arrangements on street play; parents can no longer watch their children playing and create safe havens for play. As Jane Jacobs notes in *The Death and Life of Great American Cities*, planners have much to learn from the ways in which children use their environment:

There is no point in planning for play on sidewalks unless the sidewalks are used for a wide variety of other purposes and by a wide variety of other people, too. These uses need each other, for proper surveillance, for a public life of some vitality, and for general interest. If sidewalks on a lively street are sufficiently wide, play flourishes mightily right along with other uses. If the sidewalks are skimped, rope jumping is the first play casualty. Roller skating, tricycle and bicycle riding are the next casualties. The narrower the sidewalks, the more sedentary incidental play becomes. The more frequent too become sporadic forays by children into the vehicular roadways. . . . But even when proper space is lacking, convenience of location and the interest of the streets are both so important to children—and good surveillance so important to their parents—that children will and do adapt to skimpy sidewalk space. This does not mean we do right in taking unscrupulous advantage of their adaptability. If fact, we wrong both them and cities.[16]

As Marian Wright Edelman has said, we must make the streets of our city safe for children because streets that are safe for children are safe for adults.[17] The quality of playfulness must be cared for, protected and nurtured. Children and adults need the space—both physical and emotional—to play, to develop their own indigenous arrangements and solutions and to give their imagination free rein. Brian Sutton-Smith comments on the "right of free play."[18] "The present record of children's play," he writes, "makes the point that children no less than adults live in order to live vividly, and that their play—and I would add their art—is the center of such vividness. It seems absurd to me to contrive any future playground or any school or any society in which the pursuit of such vividness is not a major focus of that construction."[19]

Clearly, people who have a control and autonomy over their environment and how it's used, and who are allowed to play with their environment, develop strong feelings of attachment to those environments—and ultimately respect them. When those attachments do not exist, they vandalize and destroy them.

Through free play, children establish bonds with their own generation; they learn about their block, about the importance of places and, ultimately, of the planet.

The memories of the many New Yorkers who have spoken with us, taken together, present a case for role of play in building multifaceted communities rooted in place; street games contributed to a neighborhood life which made growing up and living in the city memorable. We cannot turn back the clock, and, in truth, we probably can not reintroduce the games so that they will take hold again. Nor can we simply curse the modern world and paint television and organized games and sports as an ogre that would eat our children. But we must prevent these forms from becoming the predominant influence on our communities. The voice of folklorists and educators on behalf of free play must be heard alongside the pleas of reformers for organized play and the endless buzzing of the commerce-driven media.

Ultimately, we must find ways to learn from the indigenous adaptations and transformations of children and adults at play;[20] teachers must learn to encourage free play on school playgrounds; urban planners must learn to build cities children and adults can use both for work and leisure; authorities must learn the value of *casitas,* clubhouses, and other controlled spaces that city dwellers can call their own; parents must learn not to dictate but to create safe havens for play—away from the hypnotic powers of the television set. We must make a conscious effort where once none was required. As individuals, as communities, neighborhoods, cities, and nations, we must come to understand what was and is meaningful about our communities and what about them can be conserved in a changing world.

There was a game I played with Ezra so we could talk. And I don't have the faintest idea of what we talked about except that it went on forever. We talked about everything there was in the whole world. We would walk back and forth between our houses—we were walking each other home. Then finally we broke in the middle and said this has got to stop. It was two blocks and it was endless—I mean I knew that he would walk me home—and I would turn around—"Come, I'll walk you home now"—and then—"I'll walk you home." Later on it became a running joke—we discussed everything, books we'd read, politics, the world . . . where the universe was going, girls (he was more experienced than I was). It was funny, just before he died—I said, "Come on, Ezra, I'll walk you home." He smiled. He knew what I was talking about. So I walked him home. . . . I was holding his hand when his heart stopped.
Martin Pope, born 1918, Brooklyn, relating his experience growing up with children's book author Ezra Jack Keats[21]

CONCLUSION

Barbara Kirshenblatt-Gimblett

AFTERWORD: OTHER PLACES, OTHER TIMES

"The gods always play where groves are near rivers, mountains, and springs, and in towns with pleasure gardens."

FROM A HINDU TEMPLE

Arthur Leipzig

While wandering in Bhaktapur, Nepal, in January of 1984, I stumbled upon a scene that instantly conjured up Bruegel's 1559 painting of children's games. In this small city, much of its architecture dating from the late seventeenth century, open public spaces and narrow streets are stages for work, ritual, and play, all happening simultaneously. In one square, several potters were throwing clay on a large wheel, setting their wares out to harden, and tooling the drier pieces in the open. Nearby, several men were conducting an animal sacrifice at a small outdoor shrine. Townspeople passed through the square carrying materials and goods and going about their daily business. Adults and children sat, watched, and chatted; mothers supervised babies.

Knitted into this web of activity were eight to ten groups of boys and girls deeply engrossed in various play activities, within inches of the whirring potter's wheel, in the paths of pedestrians, and in small areas they had claimed for themselves. Individual boys chased hoops of various sizes, guiding the hoop with a wire. Four to six toddlers did somersaults and headstands, two formed an arch with their outstretched arms as a third child walked through, and all of them played rough and tumble on a straw mat in the open. Girls with infants strapped to their backs watched others play or joined in themselves. On the ground, a surface paved with clay tile or brick, groups of four to eight boys took advantage of exposed areas of dirt, crevices, cracks, slopes, and walls for a variety of marble games. Girls played a form of hopscotch. Elevated areas, a platform or base of a shrine, were used for play too: men shot marbles for money. Children watched others play, work, and perform the ritual sacrifice of a goat, whose decapitated body later became their toy. In another square in Bhaktapur, a man selling patent medicines had gathered round him a fascinated crowd of children and adults, while in the nearby marketplace men and women sold food and goods.

Similar scenes could be found in other Nepalese and Indian cities. In Patan, a city near Kathmandu, men played cards for money, squatting on a ledge or elevated area in the outdoors. One boy played a solitary 'board' game on a divided square scratched into a stone surface just outside a temple: he had placed small irregular stones where the lines crossed. In Bodnath, a Buddhist stuppa outside Kathmandu, men minding souvenir shops sat on crates outside the shops and played board games; nearby women did laundry or laid rice out in the sun on mats while children watched, chased hoops, and prayed. Other adults bathed or were involved in devotions and ritual offerings. Tourists passed through without any apparent disruption to the daily round of activity.

In Benares, India, the skies would fill late afternoon with paper kites flown from the banks of the Ganges or the rooftops of houses, particularly in the Moslem section of town; large trees were festooned with hundreds of pastel paper kites snagged in their branches. Marbles and hopscotch were popular activities along the riverbank, as adults made their ablutions, watered their buffalo, washed laundry, sold tea, flowers, and other goods, cleared silt from the steps near the water, prepared dung for fuel, and cremated the dead. The intensity of the urban squares, streets, and riverbanks contrasts with the quiet of the countryside surrounding the city. Improvisatory social ensembles that integrate work, ritual, and play are virtuoso performances of tacit communication in public space. They attest to the ingenuity of children and adults in organizing themselves for play purposes in so dense an environment. They give to city play its distinctive character.

In Old Delhi, pigeon flying has long been a popular sport and coops can be found on the rooftops of most houses. The skies are filled with competing flocks, and formal tournaments are organized at local and national levels. According to a recent *New York Times* article, while some men fly pigeons and others fight with cocks, partridges, bulbuls, or nightingales, Jains heal birds that are wounded or sick at their Charity Birds Hospital in Old Delhi. In accordance with their belief in the sacredness of all beings, they release healthy birds into the wild or keep the birds until they die naturally, thereby earning religious merit.[1]

At the same time, India supports the largest movie industry in the world and has created a vibrant popular culture based on modern technologies, a colonial legacy, and indigenous traditions. A rapidly growing middle class provides a ready audience for commercial amusements such as cricket matches and video bus tours.[2] Throughout the former British Empire, cricket has been picked up by local populations and in some cases, the most dramatic being the Trobriand Islands, the game has been completely transformed from a restrained competitive sport to a spectacular performance using Trobriand music, dance, and dress. Cricket is carried by emigrants to their new homes in the United States. West Indian cricket clubs play the leisurely game on hot summer weekends in Van Cortlandt Park in the Bronx. Families bring blankets and picnics and watch the game on sloping banks running parallel to the playing field. The sport even serves as the theme for a Manhattan restaurant, Cricket Club Sports Bar and Café, that serves southern Indian vegetarian food on a menu organized like a cricket game: desserts are listed under "Quicky between the Wickets" and beverages under "Caught behind the Stumps." Videotapes of cricket matches are played on a giant television screen and cricket memorabilia contribute to the decor.

". . . the world and its whole constitution is but a children's game."

JACOB CATS, *HOUWELIJK*, 1628[3]

Facing the title page of *Games and Songs of American Children* (1883) is an engraving, not of American children at play, but

AFTERWORD

CITY PLAY

of Dutch children frolicking on the streets of The Hague in the seventeenth century. They play blind man's bluff, horse and driver, leapfrog, house, and a game of tag. They roll a hoop, fly kites, play with dolls, skip rope, walk on stilts, and blow bubbles. They inflate a balloon, fly birds, straddle a rudimentary hobbyhorse, spin a top, run with a windmill, and stand on their heads. Absorbed in their own games, they are apparently oblivious to the mock militia parade winding its way down the street.[4] No doubt, William Wells Newell, compiler of this classic nineteenth-century collection of children's folklore, felt an affinity with Adriaen van de Venne, engraver of this seventeenth-century scene. Not only did both of them create an encyclopedia of children's games in city streets, but also Van de Venne's image of play in the Holland of his day is roughly contemporaneous with the founding of New Amsterdam in 1626. His engraving suggests what an intrepid folklorist might have seen on the streets of the Dutch colony.

What was it about people playing in city streets that has so fascinated commentators since antiquity? In Zechariah's utopian vision of Jerusalem under the Messiah, "the streets of the city shall be full of boys and girls playing in the streets thereof" (Zechariah 8:5). Excavations in Rome have revealed graffiti of impromptu gameboards for checkers inscribed into the ground or pavement beneath the arcades of the Basilica Iulia and the Forum.[5] In the squares and porticos of ancient Rome, people also played nut games that resemble our games of marbles; to the extent that such games encouraged gambling, they were frowned upon. During the sixteenth century, Rabelais inventoried more than two hundred play activities in Gargantua, an iconoclastic celebration of the carnivalesque, while Pieter Bruegel the Elder depicted more than ninety different games and toys in his celebrated painting of 1560, the prototype for many engravings of children's games that followed. As part of the popular culture of cities and towns, games and festivities challenged the authority of church and municipality, which tried to restrict such activities. They also offered rich iconography for moral allegory.

Granted that playing children were a menace on congested city streets: "Even in the Middle Ages, when it might be supposed a meadow was within reach of every Jack and Jill in Britain, the young had a way of gravitating to unsuitable places. In 1332, it was found necessary to prohibit boys and others from playing in the precincts of the Palace at Westminster while Parliament was sitting."[6] Laws were passed to remove certain forms of play from busy streets: "The town council statutes in Nuremberg in A.D. 1503 limited the play of marble games to a meadow outside of town."[7] Attempts to control these and other Ludic activities went beyond ridding cities and towns of a nuisance. Moral and political issues were also at stake.

Opposite: Seventeenth-century engraving by Adriaen van de Venne, frontispiece to Games and Songs of American Children *by William Wells Newell, 1883*

AFTERWORD

Historians of sixteenth-century France and Holland have explored the moral ambiguity represented by play—"the perennial conflicts between diversion and instruction, between freedom and obedience, between exploration and safety that were at the heart of contemporary attitudes towards the child."[8] In urban France, "The authorities chased all sorts of gamesters from the streets, the squares, the marketplaces, and the ramparts, where they formerly had amused themselves."[9] According to historian Robert Muchembled, repressive ordinances against ball playing, nut toss, and other gambling games, were part of a larger effort on the part of the monarchy and the church to control the popular culture of French cities, with its unruly and subversive tendencies, and make citydwellers into obedient citizens and good Catholics. A lawyer of the period, Claude de Rubys, dissented: "It is sometimes expedient to allow the people to play the fool and make merry . . . lest by holding them in with too great a rigor, we put them in despair . . ." and they turn to taverns, drink, and foment dissent, which would be far more dangerous."[10]

The urban setting of play in the literature and painting of the sixteenth and seventeenth centuries expresses not only the preoccupation with urban 'disorder,' particularly the volatility of a dense and heterogeneous population at play, and the advisability of tolerating relatively innocent ways city people let off steam. Historian Simon Schama suggests, in addition, that "by situating the games not in some imaginary vacuum of time and space, but in topographically meaningful—and sometimes recognizable— settings, nearly always with some public building, a town hall or guildhall, in view, . . . [such paintings and engravings] evoke the civic and public virtues to which the correctly brought-up child should be led."[11]

Nor can the simple playthings and pastimes that fill these city scenes escape the tendency of the time to allegorize even the humblest elements of quotidien life. Emblem books such as the one in which Van de Venne's engraving appeared in 1628, Jacob Cats's *Houwelijk,* used the metaphor of children's games for the whole world and assigned symbolic significance to kites ("hubris"), stilts ("social climbing and pretentiousness"), balloons ("inflated emptiness of earthly affairs"), and bubbles ("ephemerality of beauty and/or the fleeting character of childhood itself").[12] By the eighteenth century, those same bubbles came to signify a very different notion of childhood—one of perpetual innocence.

"Leisure in an industrial city is life itelf."

RICHARD HENRY EDWARDS, *POPULAR AMUSEMENTS,* 1915[13]

While folklorists celebrated the street as a kind of living archaeology of children's culture, social reformers at the turn of the century bemoaned the decline of home life in crowded urban neighborhoods, the unsavory nature of inner city street life, and the dangerous lure of commercial entertainments. Watching immigrants to America arrive in record numbers between 1880 and 1924 and establish neighborhoods unprecedented in their population density and cultural heterogeneity, social reformers envisioned the unravelling of an orderly and wholesome social fabric. In their characterizations of urban problems and their proposed solutions, reformers redrew the moral terrain of city play.

Their critiques reveal the workings of a bourgeois social imagination that provided Victorian ideals of respectability against which to define urban ills and their remedies. Social reformers of the late nineteenth century, particularly those attracted to the settlement movement, were often university trained and instilled with the mission of public service. In their search for a "broad region for moral adventure," settlement workers lived in the most notorious neighborhoods and sought out their most vulnerable inhabitants. Children and adolescents playing on the streets of New York's East Side, and later Harlem, became prototypical sites for their humanitarian efforts, as did the East End in London and comparable districts in other cities.

Reformers valorized the home as the center of family life, a corollary of the privatization of the domestic sphere. They expressed nostalgia for forms of community solidarity they associated with the past, the countryside, and small towns. They idealized the quiet residential street, free of hawkers, traffic, and shouting children. Reformer Michael Marks Davis, Jr., opened his 1911 study of commercial recreation in New York City with a celebration of these ideals:

> Home, sweet Home! To the well-to-do novel-reader and to our Colonial forefathers "home" meant a house big enough for a family of five, or seventeen, to sleep and eat, work and play in. All the natural activities of life centered themselves about the home, and most could express themselves within its physical limits. Consequently, home was the spiritual center of life, and, particularly for the children and adolescents, formed most of its circumference as well.
>
> How the city changes all this! The home shrinks to a nest of boxes tucked four stories in the air, or the half of a duplex house huddled upon its neighbors. There is space to sleep and eat, but not to live. The habitation becomes a sleeping box and eating den—too often no more.[14]

Due to these conditions, according to Davis, people were driven out of their "dens" and into the streets and movie palaces, at which point, reformers charged, "recreation within the modern city has become a matter of public concern; *laissez faire,* in recreation as in industry, can no longer be the policy of the state."[15] It is one thing for five hundred boys to "vent their energies upon five square miles of hill, wood and greensward around their town," where their parents can supervise them. It is quite another matter "when those five hundred must play upon a street a quarter-mile long, crowded with traffic, shops, and saloons." The "city should, and *must* have something to say about the conditions of that street."[16] Where parents have lost control of their children, their leisure and companionship, reformers demanded that the city protect their physical and moral well-being and provide for their recreation, now acknowledged to be essential to their health.

Nor did wealthier New Yorkers elude the reformers' gaze. According to Richard Henry Edwards in his 1915 report, *Popular Amusements,* the public had fallen into the "dining out habit," which he attributed to "the contracted space for the home entertainment of guests, difficulties with domestic service, and the pervading restlessness and sensationalism of city life."[17] Each class had its problems and the reformers proposed appropriate solutions. Some even idealized the play of poor children in crowded neighborhoods, which they offered as a critique of the lifestyle and pastimes of the well-to-do:

> Among all the wretched people in New York it would be hard to match the apparent wretchedness of some persons whom one sees driving in closed carriages in Central Park in winter. They look as if they never had had any fun, or known any emotion of real happiness. They look stunted and comatose. No doubt some of them are sick people; but many of them, too, are overfed and overcoddled citizens who have missed the joy of living from too great solicitude to retain the comforts of life.[18]

In contrast, one needed only visit the streets of the East Side, where "there were life, action, and social activity everywhere." Going home to respectable neighborhoods such as Murray Hill was "like returning from the land of the living to the abode of the departed. . . . Nobody in the side streets; nothing going on. Not so much light; not so good a pavement; nowhere near so much fun in sight." East Side children were said to benefit from playing with less supervision and consequently from being more "natural." Their parents were praised for being more "disciplined" by their daily labors than uptown "chappies as one may sometimes see sipping green mint and smoking cigarettes in the purlieus of the Waldorf Hotel." The sincerity and integrity of the East Siders were said to shine through the poverty and misery of their living conditions, in contrast with the "overfed, overstimulated, overamused" uptowners with their servant problems, exacting social duties, material luxuries, hypocrisy, and dejection.[19] Despite envy in some quarters for what was perceived as the freedom and spontaneity of working-class forms of sociability, most reformers were bent on inculcating the middle-class values of restraint, privacy, cultural refinement, the home-centered family, and close supervision of children.

"Not least among the deficiencies of a tenement environment is the poverty-stricken play tradition handed on to boys and girls. It would be hard to invent a commentary on a civilization more caustic than the episodes dramatized upon the streets by little children. Lady Bum and Cop, Police Patrol, Burglar, the latest crime or sex scandal, are significant not so much in their immediate vulgarity as because they are material with which mind and memory are being outfitted."

ROBERT A. WOODS AND ALBERT J. KENNEDY,
THE SETTLEMENT HORIZON, 1922 [20]

"The police here have discovered a playground stand where children operated a make-believe drug ring offering bags of grass clippings and sugar. . . . 'We just lost the war on drugs,' said Capt. Bernie Reilley. 'I don't care what Bush said, this is bad.' . . . The children recorded made-up drug transactions on a ledger and scraps of colored note paper. One note read, 'Cocaine, small half-baggie, 55 cents, small baggies, $1.'"

THE NEW YORK TIMES, AUGUST 10, 1989

What was it about city play that so alarmed the reformers? First, they feared that through the 'promiscuous' mixing of social elements in the public sphere undesirable elements would infect the whole. Warnings were sounded about "the dangers of being friendly and sociable with strangers in public places." [21] The crowd, throng, and mob, in contrast with "neighborly groups," were a repository of dark and uncontrollable forces of disorder. Reformers spoke of crowd spirit, crowd psychology, mob-mind, and mob-hysteria. [22] Social and moral evil in the form of gambling, fights, robberies, and sexual encounters was said to spread by epidemic contagion in the anarchic streets of the city: "An alley, a pocket court, or a few tenements sometimes attracts a group of sick souls who become active sources of contagion. Such nests can be disintegrated only by turning the searchlight upon them; by piling up evidence of one abomination after another that flourishes in them." [23] Commercial amusements, with their appeal to large "miscellaneous crowds," were thought "to sever the individual from the community," particularly as "bright light" districts began to draw people away from neighborhood movie houses and dance halls and into more distant entertainment districts. They feared the loss of individual will, responsibility, and moral choice. Though the regulation of amusement had been an issue in American life since at least the 1830s, the debate during the latter part of the century had to address the rise of new commercial entertainments and the massive influx of "new" immigrants, that is, people from southern and eastern Europe. [24]

Second, reformers envisioned a fragile boundary between play groups and gangs, games of chance and gambling, roughhousing and violence, pranks and vandalism, socializing and sexual promiscuity—in a word, between play and vice. Juvenile delin-

Shooting craps at Mulberry Bend, Manhattan, 1900 (Photo by George Ritter, Museum of the City of New York)

quency was of special concern. Stressing the power of play to "form the national character," reformers such as Edwards charted the relative moral value of particular leisure activities: on the "percentage of good" scale, bowling alleys rated 77.1 percent, penny arcades 38.5 percent, dance halls 23.1 percent, river excursion boats 7.7 percent, and "men only" shows 0 percent. These rankings reflected the incidence of "intemperance, obscenity, suggestions of crime, dissipation, and late hours."[25] They also reflected aesthetic and moral disgust at what was characterized as "lurid melodrama, popular songs with sappy words carried to the edge of vulgarity and linked with puerile melodies of barbarous and insistent rhythm" and a recreational atmosphere that "had become surcharged with sensuousness."[26]

Third, reformers objected to the passivity of spectating, which they contrasted with the spontaneity, originality, artfulness, and spiritual value of making your own fun: "Instead of the wholesome love of play, the love of being played upon has become a national passion."[27] They diagnosed the disease of "spectatoritis," condemned the spectacle hunter, viewed the "fan" as a parasite on the play of others, and feared the emergence of a nation of watchers.[28] Accordingly, they idealized the "amateur spirit," seeing in the professionalization of sports and the commercialization of leisure not only the passivity of spectatorship, but also a depletion of moral value. "Spontaneous" play offered an oasis of autotelic activity, undertaken for its own sake and without regard to material gain, in a world dominated by commercial transactions. Play was too important, too easily perverted, to be left to the street and marketplace.

Controlling how city people played in public was a major concern of reformers, who also sought to improve working and living conditions through protective legislation for workers, housing reform, and sanitation. Davis imagined only two "natural" settings for wholesome play, inside the home or in nature, both of them available in the New York of his day only to privileged children: "A hundred activities which in the Fifth Avenue home find their *loci* in parlor, study, den and garden, must among the mass of people be somewhere outside the limits of the home. *Where* outside, is a matter of vital importance to the public welfare."[29] That which parents do not or cannot control in the private sphere of the home, the city must control in the public spheres of park, playground, schools, and recreation centers. "Get the boys off the streets" and "Break up the gang" were rallying cries.[30]

Reformers saw the street in various ways, though recurrent metaphors include the street as the only nursery and kindergarten poor children would ever know, as a school, natural playground, impromptu dance hall, and living room.[31] For some it was bad in itself, for others the worst danger lay in its "offshoots," the doors that opened into cabarets, pool halls, saloons, and theaters. Still others saw the street itself as a shrinking playground and lamented its contraction:

AFTERWORD

Among the "human opportunities" of a district the largest of all is simply the street itself, where the tenement child spends perforce much of his time. He suffers therefrom more or less, but the normal child finds too many activities and passes too rapidly from each to each to be permanently degraded by any one. As the city congestion increases, buildings along the street grow higher, population per acre greater, traffic denser and street play less practicable. More and more commercially advantageous, therefore, become the offshoots from the street. The candy shop, as we see, is in the sequence of ages one of the first of these offshoots, and all the minor commercial provisions for recreation are similarly byways from the street—outlets for the relief of an inordinate human pressure.[32]

Distinguishing among three "natural" divisions of recreation—spontaneous, communally organized, and commercially organized—Davis characterized the tragedy of urban life in terms of the decline of spontaneous play: exhausted after work and lacking space at home to play, city people were succumbing to commercial entertainments. He proposed communally organized recreation both as a "counter-attraction" to commercial entertainments, and, paradoxically, as a way to recover "spontaneous recreation." Rather than repress play through blue laws, reformers urged that new opportunities be created for more wholesome forms of recreation, that the gymnasium, once the province of the well-to-do, be provided to all, and that parks, those quiet places where boisterous children had been unwelcome, be supplemented with playgrounds. At the same time, laws were passed to restrict street play: a report filed in 1909 indicates that thousands of children had to appear in court and could be fined because of "trivial violations, generally known as disorderly conduct. Embraced within these provisions came offenses no more serious than the playing of ball in the street, building of bon-fires, the playing of shinny and other acts growing out of the child's normal instinct for play."[33]

"True child's play is a sacred mystery, at which their elders can only obtain glances by stealth through the crevice of the curtain."

WILLIAM WELLS NEWELL,
GAMES AND SONGS OF AMERICAN CHILDREN, 1883

"I can't see any fun playing as school ma'ams say we must play."

ELEVEN-YEAR-OLD, *THE WORCESTER TELEGRAM,* 1912[34]

As early as 1883, Newell recognized the value of indigenous children's play and the futility of trying to control it:

There is something so agreeable in the idea of an inheritance of thought kept up by childhood itself, created for and adapted

Ricardo Rodriguez, the "Spanglish" rapper from "The Latin Emire," created a series of hip-hop New York scenes using plastic dolls and found objects. (Photo by Henry Chalfant)

to its own needs, that it is hard to consent to part with it. The loss cannot be made good by the deliberate invention of older minds. Children's amusement, directed and controlled by grown people, would be neither childish nor amusing. . . . Children will never adopt as their own tradition the games which may be composed or remodelled, professedly for their amusement, but with the secret purpose of moral direction.[35]

AFTERWORD

Folklorists like Newell were advocates for the traditional games and pastimes that children over the centuries had devised and urged that children be given the freedom to play as they wished. Folklorists offered their collections of children's games in support of this view.

Norman Douglas's goal in 1916 was explicitly to show the inventiveness of children in London by presenting their street games. In the process he would reveal the "stupidity of the social reformer who desires to close to the children the world of adventure, to take from them their birthright of the streets, and coop them up in well-regulated and uninspiring playgrounds where, under the supervision of teachers, their imagination will decline, their originality wither."[36] Occasionally Douglas made observations about the urban environment itself: "our boys don't much like playing in the park. . . . They prefer the streets. . . . For one thing, the keeper is always coming up in the park and interfering; next they can't find the kerbs and paving stones there; next, it makes them wild to see other boys with bats and things, when they have none."[37] He noted the vicissitudes of marbles as the police "tell the boys to move on and not block up the pavement . . . and if you don't clear off at once, they kick your marbles into the gutter where they get lost down a drain."[38]

Delighted to discover that educationalists had overlooked marbles in their efforts to organize children's games, Dorothy Howard documented the marble games of Australian children in 1954–55. "According to the memoirs of Sir Joseph Verco: 'In those days (1860–70) . . . the footpaths belonged to the small boys as much as to the city council, and they had no compunction in digging their 'nuck' holes wherever they wanted to play and neither the citizens nor the police ever interfered with their mining operations nor with their play. . . . In the nineteen-fifties, with the population concentrated more and more in city areas with more hard-surfaced playgrounds and footpaths, the old hole marble game seemed to be diminishing in favor of surface games played on diagrams of various shapes."[39]

The importance of the street to city children at play was summed up by an avid player: "When a coloured boy from Notting Hill was being given a week's vacation in a Wiltshire village, and was asked how he liked the country, he promptly replied, 'I like it—but you can't play in the road as you can in London.'"[40] Many games capitalized on the danger of the street: "It's the only really dangerous game we have, FOLLOW THE LEADER. Because of course the bravest boy is chosen as leader, one who crosses the road just in front of some heavy van and then goes and raps at all the doors of the neighbors who rush out in a rage to see what's the matter; so that by the time the third man has done the same there's sometimes a smash-up and always a row."[41] The Opies reported that "a single group of children were able to name twenty games which involved running across the road."[42]

Such games can take on a devastingly tragic character, difficult for reformers and folklorists to imagine:

> The Israeli Government is urgently trying to stop the spread
> of a deadly new game that has taken hold among the nation's
> youth. . . .
> In the first version, still played, the children lay down in a
> street or highway until a car comes. The last one to leap up and
> run away as the car gets close wins. Other children use these
> methods.
> • Place a briefcase or bag in the middle of the street, then
> dash out to pick it up as a car speeds toward it. The child who
> most narrowly misses being struck by the approaching car wins.
> • Place an Israeli candy called a "Krembo," like an American
> "Moon-pie," in the middle of the street, then dash out and grab
> it off the pavement as a car approaches. The child who gets
> closest to being hit gets to eat the candy.
> • Throw a ball into the street and chase after it as a car
> speeds forward.
> • Stand beside the street in a group, then shove one child
> from the group out in front of an approaching car and watch
> the driver try to avoid hitting him.
> • Jump into a street or crosswalk just as a car is approaching
> and stand still, to see if the driver will stop.[43]

Here, eleven- and twelve-year-old boys, growing up with the im-
minence of terrorist attack and war, explain their fascination
with the game in terms of "bravery," "tempting death," and
heroism. According to one driver, a child ran into the street after
a ball: "I braked immediately. . . . But the distance didn't allow
me to stop completely. The boy stopped and stood in the middle
of the street. I didn't understand because I expected that he
would continue to run. But no, he stood there and looked at me,
straight in the eyes. I'll never forget that look for the rest of my
life. I hit him."
This game is not new. Newell reported it in the form of Follow
Your Leader in 1883: "It is usually played out-of-doors, and the
children 'follow their leader' in a row, across roads, fences, and
ditches, jumping from heights, and creeping under barriers.
[A friend recollects how he "followed his leader" over the roofs of
houses in Boston.] We are told that the game is played in a pecu-
liarly reckless fashion in the South, where the leader will sometimes go under a horse's legs or between the wheels of a wagon,
whereupon the driver, knowing what to expect, will stop for
the rest."[44]
In their chapter on "Daring Games," the Opies acknowledge
that children learn something about risk-taking from such pastimes, but deplore their foolhardiness in courting real danger.
They also note the relationship of these tests of daring to hazing
practices. The Opies mention "Last Across," also known as "First

△ ○ △ **189** △ ○ △

to the Cemetery" and "Chicken," which is a version of the game reported in Israel. They rightly observe that "when children take part in street games it is not they who are afraid of the traffic, it is the traffic that is terrified of them; and the children are aware of this, and willing to take advantage of it."[45] During the 1950s, the British press reported "Last across the Railway Line" being played frequently throughout the Midlands to the horror of engine drivers, who then refused to drive their trains for fear of hitting a child. Variations reported then echo those seen in Israel today: "A group of children put pennies into a hat and put it down on the side of the track and the last one to move picks up the cap and claims the pennies."[46] Children were killed and injured. The Opies found accounts of the game of Chicken in the British press during the 1950s and 1960s in many of the same forms reported in Israel. Children would run bicycles through red traffic lights. They would swerve a bicycle in front of a car, jump off, lie on the ground, wait for the car to stop, and hop back on the bicycle and ride away. Or, they would lie on the road at night waiting for cars to come. One child explained that the idea of the game was "to frighten the motorist."[47]

While games of daring can offer a relatively safe context for exploring risk, games of "misplaced audacity" court real danger.[48] When such games occur among children living amid the violence of Ireland, Lebanon, Afghanistan, Israel, and other war-torn areas, they take on added significance, for they raise the question of how children at play respond to the extreme challenges posed by the violent conditions of their childhoods.

> *The street is my marae*
> *My walkman my mana*
> *My bop my blanket*
> *Keeps me warm . . .*
>
> *Polynesian Breaker,*
> *Auckland, 1980s*[49]

New York, Albuquerque, Auckland, Tokyo, London, and Berlin are the scene of a flourishing street dance scene nourished by films and music video. However much they share, the local inflections make comparison very rich. In Tokyo's Yoyogi Park adolescents gather, don fifties American clothes, black leather biker outfits, or wildly theatrical costumes, and dance to cassette tapes.[50] In Auckland, Maoris and Pacific Islanders have formed crews that breakdance in the shopping arcades, town square, schoolyards, and clubs: the Patea Maori club responded to the closing of the freezer works in the town and the massive unemployment that resulted by forming a musical group that set traditional Maori songs to disco, reggae, and other styles, cut records, and made the New Zealand charts.[51] In American cities, dance crews that were once predominantly Black or Hispanic are now ethnically mixed, as adolescents across the country take

up breakdancing. The form has even entered the fitness world, where suburban adults select between breakdancing classes and aerobics. How-to books explain the fine points of the dance form and provide basic instructions for aspiring DJs. While some party DJs sell house mix tapes on the street, others have succeeded in the commercial music industry. Recognizing that breakdancing is preferable to the fighting it supplanted, it is formally sanctioned by adults who organize competitive events, another form of control. Popular forms are even appropriated by the government for its own purposes. Disco dancing, which has become a popular form of exercise in China, is a case in point: in the weeks following the crackdown in Tiananmen Square, Chinese soldiers demonstrated disco dancing at a Beijing park as "part of a campaign to soften the army's image."[52]

Skateboarder jumping barrels, Central Park, 1980 (Photo © Martha Cooper/ City Lore)

AFTERWORD

Style, in the forms of music, dance, language, and dress, becomes a generative principle in the formation of oppositional subcultures that form around particular expressive forms, whether the centerpiece is an object (the freestyle bike, skateboard, or motorcycle), musical idiom (rock 'n' roll, heavy metal, hip-hop), or movie genre (sci-fi fans).[53] These subcultures are marked by their distinctive language, dress codes, patterns of sociability, organizations, ceremonies, musical preferences, dance forms, and diet. Describing "freestyling as a second language," an instructional booklet explains that "When two or more riders communicate in 'freestylese,' they immediately establish some common ground and are able to feel comfortable around one another. . . . New words are added and stale ones shelved on almost a daily basis. At this moment [1987], hella, aggro, and bent are in; radical, fresh, biff, and crit are out."[54] The commercial potential of these forms is exploited through instructional videos such as *Streetskating* (1988), which disseminate knowledge of the form more quickly and more widely than would be possible through the traditional conduit of oral transmission in face-to-face encounters. With each new recruit, the sales of skateboards, and the fashions and music that go with them, expand. As city streets become a playground for increasingly virtuosic skateboard performances, they also become the target of new ordinances to protect unwary pedestrians from collisions.

The street becomes the test kitchen for new urban cultural forms that in many cases are propelled beyond their immediate locale into the larger arena of mass culture. As fashion runway, the street is a dramatic showcase for displaying personal and group styles. Black hairstyles, for example, combine aesthetics, play, cultural identity, and politics:

> Nineteen Eighty-Nine. Sis Jones and I are driving a big yellow van around Brooklyn and the Bronx. . . . Everywhere we look, young black men, even finer because its summertime, are wearing crowns. Not crowns, but regal haircuts—fades, high-top fades, gumbies, slopes, high-lows, updated Jerseys and Philleys, with geometric, some call them "tribal," designs cut into the backs of their heads. . . . These heads are personal codes, calling cards. . . . Though the pride-politics behind fads may never sprout into a more coherent "movement," you got to love their attitude, their fashion stance.[55]

Byll Lester, one of the barbers responsible for the new black haircuts, sees his mission in these terms: "Integration has not worked for our communities. . . . The only way we can pull them together is through culture. If we can merchandise our culture effectively, we can change our communities."[56] Like rap music, with which these fashions are associated, the challenge is how to retain the 'outlaw' status of the forms while gaining the power of popular recognition, and how to take responsibility for that power, once it has been acquired.[57]

"In a way, Manhattan *is* Treasure Island. Its grid can be viewed as giant game [board]."

△ ○ △ 193 △ ○ △

THE LEARNING ANNEX, 1985

For running and bicycle marathons the city's roads are a racetrack. For treasure hunts and haunted tours city streets are a playing field. On a miniature golf course, the city's landmarks are toys. The Learning Annex turned "Manhattan Island into an *actual, real* gameboard for our students to seek out *fun and valuable prizes.* Master toy and game designer Todd Greenwood has created the ultimate Treasure Hunt using midtown Manhattan as the field of play." For the fee of $21, players are given clues and fan out through the streets in search of treasure. The Discovery Center, which describes itself as a lifelong learning center, features a haunted tour of New York City that resembles a slumber party for grownups in the city's streets: "The sight [*sic*] of this haunted tour will be lower Manhattan where we will visit the haunts of the haunted amid the glories of the past and the spectres of today's worldly delights." The tour includes the use of a pendulum, crystals, and ouija board to make contact with "our ethereal friends." Smelling salts are advised for the question séance that concludes the tour. The latest offerings from the Discovery Center include a Limousine Clue Chase: "Whirl around New York in luxury while searching for clues to solve an intriguing riddle! . . . Find titillating clues in such places as Central Park, South Street Seaport, Greenwich Village, and Times Square. Imagine the surprise of pedestrian by-standers when you and five other people jump out of a limo in pursuit of solving elusive riddles. . . . All teams will meet at a popular restaurant while scores are being tabulated." Alternatively, you can solve a murder on the Washington, D.C., Express, while riding Amtrak's Metroliner to and from the nation's capital. The miniature golf course currently planned by Donald Trump for Central Park will incorporate Manhattan landmarks.

Even such activities as chess acquire special meaning and form in urban settings. Chess takes a particularly urban form when played in the city's parks and streets. When Lynn Francis observed chess players in Washington Square Park, she noted the contrast between the silence that is mandatory at tournaments and clubs and the voluble patter between players and spectators in the park: "The crowd of onlookers that form around the chess tables throughout the day . . . are drawn as much, if not more, by the verbal performance of the players as by their ability at chess." As they play chess in this open outdoor park, people wander through by foot, on skateboards, skates, and bicycles, drugs are bought and sold, musicians beat drums nearby, radios and recorders blare, and traffic rumbles by. To refrain from talk would not render the play space silent. On the contrary, talk becomes the way to focus the concentration of the play group in a highly distracting environment. According to Francis, chess talk helps to define the play space, hold the group

AFTERWORD

focus, and express a play aesthetic specific to this chess world. By talking they are "fighting fire with fire."[58] The game's form, ethos, and aesthetics have been adapted to an outdoor urban space.

". . . everyday life can—and, in a sense, must—transform itself into adventure."

FRANCO MORETTI, *SIGNS TAKEN FOR WONDERS*, 1983[59]

Play as a medium of adventure infuses all aspects of city life. As "poets of their own acts," players in the city occupy space temporarily: they seize the moment to play as the opportunity arises, inserting the game into the interstices of the city's grid and schedule. In many ways, this book contributes to Michel de Certeau's exploration of "the procedures—many-sided, resilient, cunning and stubborn—that evade discipline, without thereby being outside its sphere, and that can lead to a theory of daily practices, to a theory of experienced *space* and of the disturbing familiarity of the *city*."[60] *City Play* exemplifies de Certeau's notion of "tactics": while lacking the kinds of institutions and spaces controlled by the powers that be, players transform the mundane into an adventure by means of a rope, a ball, a dance, or a haircut in spaces occupied for the moment. Those adventures lead in many directions whose paths remain to be traced.

Johnny on the pony, Brooklyn, 1950s (Photo by Arthur Leipzig)

CITY PLAY

NOTES

Preface

1. Thanks to our editor Karen Reeds for telling us this New York City joke.
2. Jonathan Goldman, *The Empire State Building Book* (New York: St. Martin's Press, 1980).
3. June Vullo, Long Island City, Queens; City Play interview, 1985.
4. Bernard Mergen, *Play and Playthings: A Reference Guide* (Westport, Conn.: Greenwood Press, 1982), p. 3.
5. Sally Banes, "Physical Graffiti—Breaking Is Hard to Do," *Village Voice,* 22–28 April 1981, p. 31.
6. Conversation with Henry Chalfant, 1989.
7. Gene Schermerhorn, *Letters to Phil: Memories of a New York Boyhood, 1848–1856,* Foreword by Brendan Gill (New York: New York Bound Books, 1982).
8. Meta Lilienthal, *Dear Remembered World: Childhood Memories of an Old New Yorker* (New York: Richard R. Smith, 1947), p. 248. Astonishingly, these memoirists (including Lilienthal) often chronicle an entire universe of memories about a New York they know is vanishing, yet neglect to mention the years that they cover; future readers scour for clues to the dates of their childhoods.
9. Carole Baer, Yorkville, Manhattan; City Play interview, 1984.
10. Benjamin Chiaro, Jr., born 1947, Hoboken, New Jersey; City Play interview, 1984.
11. Brian Sutton-Smith, *A History of Children's Play: The New Zealand Playground, 1840–1950* (Philadelphia: University of Pennsylvania Press, 1981), p. 296.
12. Mergen, *Play and Playthings,* p. ix.
13. Philippe Ariès, *Centuries of Childhood* (New York: Knopf, 1962).

Introduction: Play in the Urban Environment

1. Yi-Fu Tuan, *Space and Place: The Perspective of Experience* (Minneapolis: University of Minnesota Press, 1977), pp. 17, 18.
2. Michael Licht, born 1949, Lower East Side, Manhattan; City Play interview, 1984.
3. Marie Stock, born 1925, Washington Heights, Manhattan; City Play interview, 1984.
4. Martha Verna, born 1910, the Bronx; City Play interview, 1987.
5. For categorizations of different kinds of games and play see Roger Callois, *Man, Play, and Games* (New York: The Free Press, 1961); John M. Roberts, M. J. Arth, and R. R. Bush, "Games in Culture," *American Anthropologist* 61 (1959): 597–605.
6. David Nasaw, *Children of the City: At Work and at Play* (Garden City, N.Y.: Anchor Press/Doubleday, 1985), p. vii.
7. Michael Winkleman, *The Fragility of Turf: The Neighborhoods of New York City* (Albany: New York State Education Department, New York State Museum, Division of Research and Collections, 1986), p. 1.

8. Martin Heidegger, "An Ontological Consideration of Place," in *The Question of Being* (New York: Twayne Publishers, 1958), p. 24.

9. Susan Elizabeth Lyman, *The Story of New York: An Informal History of the City from the First Settlement to the Present Day* (New York: Crown Publishers, 1975), pp. 5, 6.

10. Ibid., p. 6.

11. Winkleman, *The Fragility of Turf,* pp. 1, 3.

12. Abe Lass, born 1907, Flatbush, Brooklyn; City Play interviews, 1988.

13. Winkleman, *The Fragility of Turf,* p. 2.

14. Ibid.

15. George Herland, *Centuries of Childhood in New York: A Celebration on the Occasion of the 275th Anniversary of Trinity School* (New York: The New-York Historical Society and Trinity School, 1984), p. 21.

16. Jacob Riis, *Children of the Poor* (New York: Charles Scribner's Sons, 1892).

17. Lyman, *Story of New York,* p. 189.

18. Winkleman, *The Fragility of Turf,* p. 5.

19. Susan Mildred Brown, 1940s and '50s, Central Park South and West, Manhattan; City Play interview, 1984.

20. Parnell Jones, born 1901, Harlem, Manhattan; City Play interview, 1984.

21. Robert Paul Smith, *"Where Did You Go?" "Out" "What Did You Do?" "Nothing"* (New York: W. W. Norton and Co., 1957), p. 33.

22. Sylvia Lass, born 1915, Lower East Side, Manhattan; City Play interview, 1986.

23. *New York Tribune* (July 5, 1896); quoted in Allon Schoener, *Portal to America: The Lower East Side, 1870–1925* (New York: Holt, Rinehart and Winston, 1967), p. 68.

24. Schermerhorn, *Letters to Phil,* p. 15.

25. Zachary Summers, born 1929, Brownsville and Sheepshead Bay, Brooklyn; City Play interview, 1985.

26. For a dramatic example of a traffic accident involving a horse and wagon, see Michael Gold, *Jews Without Money* (1930; rpt., New York: Carroll & Graf Publishers, Inc., 1984), pp. 48, 49.

27. Alice Havlena, born 1911, Astoria, Queens; City Play interview, 1982.

28. For a discussion of the changing differences between the play of boys and girls, see Brian Sutton-Smith, "Sixty Years of Historical Change in the Game Preferences of American Children," in *The Folkgames of Children* (Austin: University of Texas Press/American Folklore Society, 1972), pp. 258–311.

29. Sophie Ruskay, *Horsecars and Cobblestones* (1948; rpt., Cranbury, N.J.: A. S. Barnes and Company, 1973), p. 41.

30. Francine Kern, born 1932, Richmond Hill, Queens; City Play correspondence, August 1984.

31. Susan Namm, born 1939, Crown Heights and Flatbush, Brooklyn; City Play interview, 1985.

32. City Play Fieldnotes, 1985, City Lore, The New York Center for Urban Folk Culture, New York, N.Y.

33. Told to Steven Zeitlin in conversation at a meeting of The Anthropological Association for the Study of Play, 1984.

34. City Play interview with Mary Scherbatskoy, co-director, ARTS, Inc., August 1989 (Arts Resources for Teachers conducts oral history and folklife

NOTES

projects with school-age children in Chinatown and the Lower East Side of Manhattan).

35. Lilienthal, *Dear Remembered World*, p. 25.
36. Abe Lass, born 1907, Flatbush, Brooklyn; City Play interview, 1984.
37. Henry Roth, *Call It Sleep* (1934; rpt. New York, Avon Books, 1964).
38. Ben Swedowsky, born 1926, East Harlem, Manhattan; City Play interview, 1984.
39. Henry Adams, *The Education of Henry Adams* (New York: The Modern Library, 1931), p. 42, quoted in Mergen, *Play and Playthings*, p. 29.
40. Mergen, *Play and Playthings*, p. 30.
41. Guy Trebay, "Wild Style," *Village Voice* (June 17, 1986), p. 71.
42. Susan Mildred Brown, 1940s and '50s, Central Park South and West, Manhattan; City Lore segment of WNYC's "New York and Company," July 29, 1988.
43. John Camonelli, born 1919, East Harlem, Manhattan; City Play interview, 1984.
44. Barbara Kirshenblatt-Gimblett, "Urban Play," unpublished manuscript, 1989.
45. Emily Vanderpoel, ed., *More Chronicles of a Pioneer School: From 1792 to 1833* (New York: Cadmus Book Shop, 1927), p. 185; quoted in Mergen, *Play and Playthings*, p. 17.
46. Quoted in *Child: A Literary Companion,* ed. Helen Handley and Andra Samelson (Wainscott, N.Y.: Pushcart Press, 1988), p. 85.
47. Johan Huizinga, *Homo Ludens: A Study of the Play Element in Culture* (London: Routledge and Kegan Paul, 1949; Boston: Beacon Press, 1955), p. 13.
48. Mergen, *Play and Playthings,* p. 5.
49. Erving Goffman, "Fun in Games," in *Encounters* (Indianapolis: Bobbs-Merrill, 1961).
50. Mihaly Csiszentmihalyi, *Flow Studies of Enjoyment* (PHS Grant Report, University of Chicago, 1974).
51. Barbara Biber, "What Play Means to Your Child," unpublished manuscript, p. 1.
52. Smith, *"Where Did You Go?" "Out" "What Did You Do?" "Nothing,"* p. 99.
53. Jeff Warner, "Songs and Stories about Death" (Lecture at the Philadelphia Museum of Art, March, 1979).
54. Sutton-Smith, *A History of Children's Play,* p. 297.
55. Bess Lomax Hawes (Lecture, American Studies Department, George Washington University, 1978).
56. William Wells Newell, *Games and Songs of American Children* (1883; rpt., New York: Dover Publications, 1963), p. 70.
57. Ibid.
58. Barbara Kirshenblatt-Gimblett, "Urban Play," unpublished manuscript, pp. 5, 6.
59. Newell, *Games and Songs of American Children,* p. 70.
60. Lawrence Levine, *Black Culture and Black Consciousness* (New York: Oxford University Press, 1977), p. 198; quoted in Mergen, *Play and Playthings,* p. 48.
61. See Kate Rinzler, *1974 Festival of American Folklife* (Washington, D.C.: Smithsonian Institution, 1974).
62. Alice Bertha Gomme, *The Traditional Games of England, Scotland, and*

NOTES

Ireland, 2 vols. (1894, 1898; rpt., New York: Dover Publications, 1964).

63. Norman Douglas, *London Street Games* (1916; rpt., London: Chatto and Windus, 1931; rpt., New York: Johnson Reprint Corporation in 1969).

64. See Herbert Halpert, "Folk Rhymes of New York City Children" (Master's thesis, Columbia University, 1946); Harlem children's rhymes recorded by Ralph Ellison at the playground at East 139th Street and Lenox Avenue, New York City, 1939 (Manuscripts of the Federal Writers' Project of the Works Progress Administration, deposited in the Folklore Section, Library of Congress, Washington, D.C.).

65. See Iona and Peter Opie, *Children's Games in Street and Playground* (Oxford: Clarendon Press, 1969).

66. Mary and Herbert Knapp, *One Potato, Two Potato . . . : The Secret Education of American Children* (New York: W.W. Norton and Co., 1976).

67. Simon J. Bronner, *American Children's Folklore* (Little Rock, Ark.: August House, 1988).

68. Brooklyn, City Play interview, 1988.

69. Gary Alan Fine, "Children and Their Culture: Exploring Newell's Paradox," *Western Folklore* 39, no. 3 (July 1980), 170–183.

70. Bess Lomax Hawes, "Law and Order on the Playground," in *Games in Education and Development,* ed. Loyda M. Shears and Eli M. Bower (Springfield, Ill.: Charles C. Thomas, 1974), pp. 13, 16, 170–183.

71. Ethel and Oliver Hale, "From Sidewalk, Gutter and Stoop: Being a Chronicle of Children's Play and Game Activity," New York, 1938, manuscript, New York Public Library, 2 packages.

INCORPORATION

1. Maxine Miska and I. Sheldon Posen, *Tradition and Community in the Urban Neighborhood: Making Brooklyn Home* (New York: Brooklyn Education and Cultural Alliance, 1983), p. 9.

2. Joan Radnor, born 1944, Manhattan; City Play interview, 1984.

3. John Camonelli, born 1919, East Harlem, Manhattan; City Play interview, 1984.

4. Walter Noonan, Transit Museum interview, NC7-89, City Lore, Manhattan and New York Transit Museum, Brooklyn.

5. Miska and Posen, *Tradition and Community in the Urban Neighborhood,* pp. 10, 11.

6. See Martha Cooper and Henry Chalfant, *Subway Art* (New York: Holt, Rinehart and Winston, 1984).

7. George Burns, *Third Time Around;* quoted in Nasaw, *Children of the City,* p. 30.

8. Don Fellman, born 1949, Long Island City, Queens; City Play interview, 1987.

9. Fred Ferretti, "City Games," in *1976 Festival of American Folklife,* ed. Bess Hawes (Washington, D.C.: Smithsonian Institution, 1976), p. 31.

10. Jimmy Savo, *I Bow to the Stones: Memories of a New York Childhood* (New York: Howard Frisch, 1963), p. 73.

11. Marsha Zeusse, born 1937, Bay Ridge, Brooklyn; City Play interview, 1984.

12. Henry Noble MacCracken, *Family on Gramercy Park* (New York: Charles Scribner's Sons, 1949), p. 138.

13. Abe Lass, born 1907, Flatbush, Brooklyn, City Play interview, 1984.

14. The City Play interviews are archived and accessible either through City Lore: The New York Center for Urban Folk Culture (72 East First Street, New York, New York 10003) or Queens Council on the Arts (161–04 Jamaica Avenue, Jamaica, New York 11432). The locations listed in the manuscript refer to the places where our informants grew up, and where the episodes they recounted took place, not necessarily to their birthplaces.

15. Opening Address by Luis E. Figueroa, Unitarian Church of All Souls, Manhattan, 1988.

16. Barbara Kirshenblatt-Gimblett, "Urban Play," unpublished manuscript, 1989, p. 23.

17. John Collier and Edward M. Barrows, *The City Where Crime Is Play: The People's Institute of New York* (New York, 1914); quoted in Cary Goodman, *Choosing Sides: Playground and Street Life on the Lower East Side* (New York: Schocken Books, 1979), p. 12.

18. Roger Hart, *Children's Experience of Place* (New York: Irvington Publishers, 1979), pp. 57–67; quoted in Mergen, *Play and Playthings,* p. 86.

19. Gaston Bachelard, *The Poetics of Space,* trans. Maria Jolas (1958; rpt., Boston: Beacon Press, 1964).

20. Euphemia Mason Olcott, "Personal Recollections of Greenwich Village," *Bruno's Weekly,* April 22, 1916; quoted in Herland, *Centuries of Childhood in New York,* p. 47.

21. Lockwood, *Bricks and Brownstone,* p. xiii.

22. Charles B. Lawlor and James W. Blake, "The Sidewalks of New York" ("East Side, West Side, All Around the Town"), 1894.

23. Conversation with architectural historian and writer, Andrew Dolkart, 1987.

24. Lockwood, *Bricks and Brownstone,* p. xiii.

25. Ibid., pp. 10, 11.

26. Ibid.

27. Lilienthal, *Dear Remembered World,* pp. 63, 64.

28. "Light Up, New York: Streetlighting in the Era of Electricity," exhibition, Municipal Art Society, Manhattan, 1989.

29. Lilienthal, *Dear Remembered World,* p. 64.

30. James F. Carey, Fireman, Engine 267, "Hydrant History: History of The Fire Hydrant Traced from the Wooden Plug to Modern High Pressure System" *W.N.Y.F.* (July 1946), p. 30.

31. Colin Ward, *A Child in the City* (New York: Pantheon Books, 1978), p. 83.

32. Ethel and Oliver Hale, "From Sidewalk, Gutter and Stoop," p. 335.

33. Carole King, "Up on the Roof," Warner Bros.–7 Arts Records, Screengems Music, EMI Music Corp., Secaucus, N.J., 1962.

34. Jane Schwartz, "The Pigeon Game: The Pleasures of a Little-Known Rooftop Sport," *Quest* (November 1980), p. 56.

35. Miska and Posen, *Tradition and Community in the Urban Neighborhood,* p. 13.

36. Ibid., p. 13.

37. Schwartz, "The Pigeon Game," p. 56.

38. Miska and Posen, *Tradition and Community in the Urban Neighborhood,* p. 13.

NOTES

39. Jane Schwartz, *Caught* (New York: Available Press/Ballantine Books, 1985), pp. 147, 148.
40. Barbara Kirshenblatt-Gimblett, "The Future of Folklore Studies in America: The Urban Frontier," *Folklore Forum* 16 (Fall 1983), p. 186.
41. Smith, *"Where Did You Go?" "Out" "What Did You Do?" "Nothing,"* p. 60.
42. Ibid.
43. Gold, *Jews Without Money,* pp. 45, 46, 48.
44. Guy Trebay, "Wild Style," *Village Voice,* June 17, 1986, p. 71.
45. John Barbour, *Long Island Press,* 1966.
46. Abe Lass, born 1907, Flatbush, Brooklyn; WNYC "Senior Edition" radio show, Children's Games, 1985.
47. Nasaw, *Children of the City,* p. 117.
48. Isaac Asimov, *In Memory Yet Green: The Autobiography of Isaac Asimov, 1920–1954* (Garden City, N.Y.: Doubleday & Company, 1979), p. 64.
49. Ethel and Oliver Hale, "From Sidewalk, Gutter and Stoop."
50. Schermerhorn, *Letters to Phil,* p. 16.
51. Mary Douglas, *Purity and Danger* (New York: Chapman, Routledge and Hall, 1984).
52. Riis, *Children of the Poor,* p. 69.
53. Ibid.
54. Ibid., p. 70.
55. Ibid., p. 66.
56. Hamilton Fish Armstrong, *Those Days* (New York: Harper & Row, 1963), pp. 61, 62, 76.
57. Contributed anonymously to Steven Zeitlin, Amy Kotkin, and Holly Cutting Baker, *A Celebration of American Family Folklore* (New York: Pantheon Books, 1982), p. 173.
58. *New York Tribune* (July 5, 1896), quoted in Schoener, *Portal to America,* p. 68.
59. Don Fellman, born 1949, Long Island City, Queens; City Play interviews, 1984–1989.
60. Mergen, *Play and Playthings,* p. 220.
61. Richard Wallace, born 1949, Philadelphia; City Play interview, 1989.
62. Sutton-Smith, *A History of Children's Play,* pp. 272, 273.
63. Bill Cosby, "Street Football," *The Best of Bill Cosby,* Warner Brothers–Seven Arts Records, Inc. By permission of Bill Cosby and Turtle Head Publishing Company.
64. Sutton-Smith, *A History of Children's Play,* pp. 273.
65. Schermerhorn, *Letters to Phil,* p. 17.
66. William M. Firshing, *A Boy Grows in Brooklyn* (Tampa: American Studies Press, 1987), p. 11.
67. *New York Times* (July 30, 1989), p. 47.
68. See Samuel Lee, *Rapping with the Rappers,* three-quarter-inch videotape, Queens Council on the Arts, 1986.
69. Ethel and Oliver Hale, "From Sidewalk, Gutter and Stoop."
70. Michael Marks Davis, Jr., *The Exploitation of Pleasure: A Study of Commercial Recreation in New York City* (New York: Russell Sage Foundation, Department of Child Hygiene, 1911), p. 5.
71. Nasaw, *Children of the City,* p. 34.
72. Cooper and Chalfant, *Subway Art,* p. 39.
73. Ward, *A Child in the City.*

NOTES

74. Willie Sutton, with Edward Linn, *Where the Money Was: The Memoirs of a Bank Robber* (New York: Viking Press, 1976).

75. Ethel and Oliver Hale, "From Sidewalk, Gutter and Stoop," p. 461.

76. Schermerhorn, *Letters to Phil,* pp. 33, 34.

77. Havens, *Diary of a Little Girl in Old New York,* diary entry for December 10, 1849, p. 51.

78. Lilienthal, *Dear Remembered World,* p. 52.

79. Gold, *Jews Without Money,* p. 41.

80. Charles Haynes Haswell, *Reminiscences of an Octagenarian of the City of New York (1816–1860)* (New York: Harper & Bros. Publ., 1897), p. 77.

81. Donald Knowler, "The Pleasures of Central Park," *The New York Times Magazine* (December 25, 1983), p. 13.

TRANSFORMATION

1. Steven Smith, *Blind Zone* (Toronto, Canada: Aya Press, 1987).

2. Gregory Bateson, "A Theory of Play and Fantasy," American Psychiatric Association, *Psychiatric Research Reports 2* (December 1955); reprinted in *Steps to an Ecology of Mind* (New York: Ballantine, 1972), pp. 177–193.

3. We are indebted to Barbara Kirshenblatt-Gimblett for this observation.

4. Ethel and Oliver Hale, "From Sidewalk, Gutter and Stoop," p. 97.

5. Nasaw, *Children of the City,* p. 99.

6. Sam Levenson, *Everything But Money* (New York: Pocket Books, 1967, p. 83).

7. Mary Jo, [informant did not supply her last name], born 1964, Astoria, Queens; City Play interview, 1984.

8. Henry Chalfant and Tony Silver, *Style Wars,* 16mm documentary, New Day Films, 1985.

9. City Play interview, 1989, with Mary Scherbatskoy, co-director of ARTS, Inc., which conducts folklore and oral history projects in Chinatown and the Lower East Side of New York.

10. Queens Council on the Arts interview with Henry Callejo, Astoria, Queens, 1982.

11. Miska and Posen, *Tradition and Community in the Urban Neighborhood,* p. 27.

12. Edward Brophy, born 1937, Upper West Side, Manhattan; interview on WNYC's "New York and Company," July 29, 1988. See also Edward Brophy, "Street Lore," unpublished manuscript.

13. Haswell, *Reminiscences of an Octagenarian,* p. 77.

14. John Prine, "Far from Me," Walden Music/Sour Grapes Music, 1971.

15. Havens, *Diary of a Little Girl in Old New York,* p. 51.

16. Mergen, *Play and Playthings,* p. 83.

17. Mary Crosby, "Reminiscences of Rutgers Place written for May F. Jones by her Great-Aunt, Mary Crosby."

18. Susan Mildred Brown, 1940s and '50s, Central Park South, Manhattan; City Play interview, 1984.

19. We are indebted to Barbara Kirshenblatt-Gimblett and Jack Kugelmass for this observation.

20. Kirshenblatt-Gimblett, "The Future of Folklore Studies in America," p. 186.

21. Ibid.

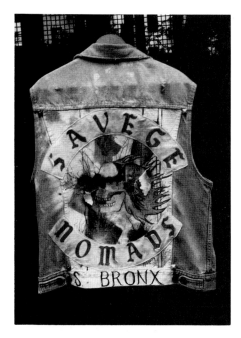

22. Ethel and Oliver Hale, "From Sidewalk, Gutter and Stoop," p. 111.
23. Interview by Joseph Sciorra, City Lore, Brooklyn, 1985.

CONTROL

1. Sutton-Smith, *The Folkgames of Children,* p. xiii.
2. City Play Fieldnotes, Amanda Dargan, 1985.
3. Julius Sokolsky, born 1925, the Bronx; City Play interview, 1988.
4. Susan Mildred Brown, 1940s and '50s, Central Park South and West, Manhattan; City Play interview, 1984.
5. Research on the Brooklyn Elite Checker Club was conducted by Dr. Susan Slyomovics in the early 1980s.
6. Kirshenblatt-Gimblett, "The Future of Folklore Studies in America," pp. 196, 197.
7. William E. Geist, "About New York: A Spot for 'Millionaires' in Spanish Harlem," *New York Times* (Oct. 26, 1985), section L, p. 31.
8. City Play Fieldnotes, I. Sheldon Posen, 1986.
9. Kirshenblatt-Gimblett, "The Future of Folklore Studies in America," pp. 196, 197.
10. Fieldnotes, Joseph Sciorra, City Lore's Ethnic Social Clubs Project.
11. Geoffrey Biddle "Alphabet City," unpublished manuscript, 1989.
12. Kirshenblatt-Gimblett, "The Future of Folklore Studies in America," pp. 196, 197.
13. Suzanne Wasserman, "Clubs, Cafés, Corners and Candy Stores: Youth Leisure-Time Culture on the Lower East Side during the Depression," draft of doctoral dissertation.
14. Emeric Kurtagh and George Stoney, "Rooms of Their Own: A Survey of 28 Lower East Side Social Clubs," June 1939, Henry Street Settlement, pp. 7, 40, 46; quoted in Wasserman, "Clubs, Cafés, Corners and Candy Stores," p. 21.
15. Fieldnotes, Joseph Sciorra, City Lore's Ethnic Social Clubs Project, August 1988.
16. Edward Brophy, born 1937, Upper West Side, Manhattan; City Play interview, 1987.
17. Ellen Summers, 1930s and '40s, Coney Island, Brooklyn.
18. Peter Melia, born 1937, Bay Ridge, Brooklyn; City Play interview, 1984.
19. Nasaw, *Children of the City,* p. 37.
20. Lloyd E. Ohlin and Richard A. Cloward, *Delinquency and Opportunity: A Theory of Delinquent Gangs* (Glencoe, Ill.: The Free Press, 1960).
21. MacCracken, *Family on Gramercy Park,* pp. 48–67.
22. Gold, *Jews Without Money,* pp. 42, 43.
23. Ward, *A Child in the City,* p. 116.
24. Sophie Degner, born 1902, East New York, Manhattan; City Play interview, 1984.
25. Ethel and Oliver Hale, "From Sidewalk, Gutter and Stoop," pp. 5, 6.
26. Gold, *Jews Without Money,* p. 70.
27. Viviana Zelizer *Pricing the Priceless Child: The Changing Social Value of Children* (New York: Basic Books, 1985), p. 41.
28. Ethel and Oliver Hale, "From Sidewalk, Gutter and Stoop," p. 11.
29. Savo, *I Bow to the Stones,* pp. 55, 56.
30. Zelizer, *Pricing the Priceless Child,* p. 53.
31. Abe Lass, born 1907, Flatbush, Brooklyn; City Play interview, 1984.
32. Wald, *House on Henry Street,* p. 71.

NOTES

33. See Kirshenblatt-Gimblett, "Urban Play," unpublished manuscript, 1989, p. 6.
34. Dominick Cavallo, *Muscles and Morals: Organized Playgrounds and Urban Reform, 1880–1920* (Philadelphia: University of Pennsylvania Press, 1981), p. 43.
35. Information supplied by the Police Athletic League.
36. Interview with Detective David Walker, president of the American Double Dutch League, by Kay Sloman, December 2, 1983.
37. Mergen, *Play and Playthings,* pp. 57, 58.
38. June Goodwin, "Double Dutch, Double Dutch: All You Need Is a Clothesline and Jet-Propelled Feet," *The Christian Science Monitor,* October 7, 1980; quoted in Kirshenblatt-Gimblett, "The Future of Folklore Studies in America," p. 205.
39. Kirshenblatt-Gimblett, "The Future of Folklore Studies in America," p. 206.
40. Ibid.
41. Mary and Herbert Knapp, *One Potato, Two Potato . . . ,* p. 267.
42. Khadijah Shaheed, born 1958, Bedford-Stuyvesant, Brooklyn; City Play interview, 1984.

CONCLUSION: A COMMUNITY ROOTED IN PLACE

1. Steven Saraband, 1950 and '60s, the Bronx; City Play interview, 1985.
2. Gaston Bachelard, *The Poetics of Reverie: Childhood, Language, and the Cosmos,* trans. Daniel Russell (1960; rpt., Boston: Beacon Press, 1971), p. 20.
3. Charles J. Zerner, "The Street Hearth of Play: Children in the City," *Landscape* 22 (Autumn 1977) 21, 23.
4. Ethel and Oliver Hale, "From Sidewalk, Gutter and Stoop," p. 77.
5. Sutton-Smith, *A History of Children's Play,* p. 288.
6. Ibid., pp. 248, 249.
7. "New Yorkers Replay Games of Childhood in a Far Clime," *New York Times,* September 30, 1985.
8. Brian Sutton-Smith, *Children's Play, Past, Present and Future* (Philadelphia: Please Touch Museum, 1985), p. 4.
9. Thanks to Mary Hufford for this insightful observation.
10. Kirshenblatt-Gimblett, "Urban Play," unpublished manuscript, 1989, pp. 40, 41.
11. City Play interview with Henry Chalfant, August 1989.
12. Armstrong, *Those Days,* p. 76.
13. Don Fellman, born 1949, Long Island City, Queens; City Play interview, 1984.
14. Ward, *A Child in the City.*
15. Zerner, "The Street Hearth of Play," p. 30.
16. Jane Jacobs, *The Death and Life of Great American Cities* (New York, Knopf, 1961).
17. Marian Wright Edelman, Sermon at the Unitarian Church of All Souls, Manhattan, 1987.
18. Sutton-Smith, *Children's Play: Past, Present and Future,* p. 19.
19. Sutton-Smith, *A History of Children's Play,* p. 297.
20. Kirshenblatt-Gimblett, "Urban Play," unpublished manuscript, 1989.
21. Martin Pope, born 1918, East New York; City Play interview, 1985.

NOTES

AFTERWORD

I would like to thank the International School of America for making it possible for me to observe city play in India and Nepal.

1. Steven R. Wiseman, "In Old Delhi: A Hospital for Fighting Nightingales," *New York Times* (April 4, 1986), A2.

2. Arjun Appadurai, "Imagined Worlds: Cricket and the Decolonization of the Production of Culture" (Paper presented at the 16th Annual Conference on South Asia, Madison, Wisconsin, November 6–8, 1987).

3. Quoted in Simon Schama, *The Embarrassment of Riches: An Interpretation of Dutch Culture in the Golden Age* (Berkeley: University of California Press, 1988), p. 499.

4. The entire topos of "children's games" in Dutch painting and prints of the sixteenth and seventeenth centuries is discussed by Schama, *The Embarrassment of Riches,* pp. 497–516. He cites the relevant recent literature on Bruegel and his followers. I am indebted to his analysis.

5. Jérôme Carcopino, *Daily Life in Ancient Rome,* trans. E. O. Lorimer (New Haven: Yale University Press, 1940), pp. 252–253: "When the players felt chess to be too complicated or the necessary apparatus for it too cumbersome—a chess-board of sixty squares and men of different colour and shape—they would fall back on an elementary game of draughts, whose *tabulae lusoriae* could be improvised anywhere with lines scratched in the ground or cut into the pavement." According to Carcopino, over one hundred such gameboards have been found; children playing nut games can be seen on bas-reliefs.

6. Iona and Peter Opie, *Children's Games,* p. 11.

7. E. M. Avedon and Brian Sutton-Smith, eds., *The Study of Games* (New York: John Wiley, 1971), p. 22.

8. Schama, *The Embarrassment of Riches,* p. 499.

9. Robert Muchembled, *Popular Culture and Elite Culture in France 1400–1750,* trans. Lydia Cochrane (Baton Rouge: Louisiana State University Press, 1985), p. 164.

10. Quoted by Natalie Davis, "The Reasons of Misrule," *Society and Culture in Early Modern France* (Stanford: Stanford University Press, 1975), p. 97.

11. Schama, *The Embarrassment of Riches,* p. 499.

12. Ibid., p. 515.

13. Richard Henry Edwards, *Popular Amusements* (New York: Association Press, 1915), Studies in American Social Conditions 8. I would like to thank Minda Novek for bringing this source, as well as Davis, *Exploitation of Pleasure,* to my attention.

14. Davis, *The Exploitation of Pleasure,* p. 3.

15. Ibid., p. 4. Davis is echoing ideas put forward by Washington Gladden, who was already writing on the uses and abuses of amusements in the 1860s, and by contemporaries of Davis, such as Theodore Munger.

16. Ibid., pp. 3–4.

17. Edwards, *Popular Amusements,* p. 68.

18. E. S. Martin, "East Side Considerations," *Harper's New Monthly Magazine* (1898).

19. Ibid.

20. Robert A. Woods and Albert J. Kennedy, *The Settlement Horizon: A National Estimate* (New York: Russell Sage Foundation, 1922).

NOTES

21. Edwards, *Popular Amusements*, p. 70.

22. There are echoes here of the popular book *The Crowd*, by Gustave Le Bon, which was first published in French in 1895.

23. Woods and Kennedy, *Settlement Horizon*, pp. 307–308.

24. Edwards, *Popular Amusements*, p. 139. See also Ernest W. Burgess, "Can Neighborhood Work Have a Scientific Basis?" in *The City*, by Robert E. Park, Ernest W. Burgess, and Roderick D. McKenzie (1925; rpt., Chicago: University of Chicago Press, 1967), pp. 142–155. The conference "Inventing Times Square" (New York Institute for the Humanities, 1989) dealt with these issues: see, in particular, Richard Wightman Fox, "The Discipline of Amusement," and Peter G. Buckley, "More Boundaries of Respectibility."

25. Edwards, *Popular Amusements*, pp. 24, 20.

26. Woods and Kennedy, *The Settlement Horizon*, p. 101.

27. Edwards, *Popular Amusements*, p. 134.

28. See, for example, Edwards, *Popular Amusements*, pp. 134 ff and J. B. Nash, *Spectatoritis* (New York, 1932).

29. Davis, *Exploitation of Pleasure*, p. 4.

30. See, for example, Woods and Kennedy, *The Settlement Horizon*, p. 73.

31. See Bella Mead, "The Social Pleasures of the East Side Jews" (Master's thesis, Columbia University, 1904), p. 5; Edith Davids, "The Kindergarten of the Streets," *Everybody's Magazine* (1903); and more recently Janet Abu-Lughod, "Tompkins Square," REALM (Research about the Lower East Side) Occasional Papers #1 (New York: New School for Social Research, 1988). Consider the street as domestic interior in relation to the current discourse on "homelessness," as well as in middle-class neighborhoods. On Saturdays in warm weather in the Hasidic communities of Borough Park, the streets become an extension of the interior, the porch, balcony, and front yard: men sit in shirtsleeves reading on the balcony, while women in their housecoats, slippers, and kerchiefs (wigs have been put aside) socialize on the street.

32. Davis, *Exploitation of Pleasure*, p. 45.

33. Cary Goodman, *Choosing Sides: Playground and Street Life on the Lower East Side* (New York: Schocken Books, 1979), p. 15.

34. Quoted by Roy Rozenzweig, *Eight Hours for What You Will: Workers and Leisure in an Industrial City, 1870–1920* (Cambridge: Cambridge University Press), p. 151.

35. Newell, *Games and Songs*, p. 12.

36. Norman Douglas, *London Street Games* (1916; rpt., London: Chatto and Windus, 1931; New York: Johnson Reprint Corporation, 1969), p. xi.

37. Ibid., p. 61.

38. Ibid., p. 63.

39. Dorothy Howard, "Marble Games of Australian Children," in Avedon and Sutton-Smith, *The Study of Games* (reprinted from *Folklore* 71 [1960]: 165–179), pp. 180–181.

40. Opie, *Children's Games*, p. 10.

41. Douglas, *London Street Games*, p. 78.

42. Opie, *Children's Games*, p. 11.

43. Joel Brinkley, "Lethal Game of 'Chicken' Emerges for Israeli Boys," *The New York Times*, April 3, 1989, p. A2.

44. Newell, *Games and Songs*, p. 122. The Opies, in *Children's Games*, p. 266,

NOTES

suggest that daring games of various kinds can be found as early as the seventeenth century among adults in England.

45. Opie, *Children's Games,* p. 269.

46. *Yorkshire Post* (April 28, 1961), p. 9, quoted in Opie, *Children's Games,* p. 269.

47. Opie, *Children's Games,* p. 271.

48. Ibid., p. 272.

49. Mark Scott, *Street Action Aotearoa* (Auckland, New Zealand: Arohanui Publications, 1985), p. [3]. Bop is the New Zealand term for breakdancing and related forms, mana is a Polynesian word for prestige, and marae refers to the ceremonial center of the Maori, where local gatherings are held and rituals conducted. I am indebted to Bridget Ikin for providing me with a copy of this publication.

50. See C. Scott Littleton, "Tokyo Rock and Roll," *Natural History* 94, 8 (August 1985): 48–57.

51. See Scott, *Street Action.*

52. "Chinese Soldiers Dance for a New Image," *The New York Times* (July 26, 1989), p. A3.

53. See for example, William Graebner, *Coming of Age in Buffalo: Teenage Culture in the Postwar Era* (Buffalo: Buffalo and Erie County Historical Society, 1986); Dick Hebdige, *Subculture: The Meaning of Style* (London: Methuen, 1979); Michael Brake, *Comparative Youth Culture: The Sociology of Youth Cultures and Youth Subcultures in America, Britain, and Canada* (London: Routledge & Kegan Paul, 1985); David Toop, *The Rap Attack: African Jive to New York Hip Hop* (London: Pluto Press, 1984); and Iain Chambers, *Popular Culture: The Metropolitan Experience* (London: Methuen, 1986).

54. Don Toshach, *Freestyling* (New York: Perigree Books, 1987), p. 13.

55. Lisa Jones, "Fade to Black," *Village Voice* (August 1, 1989), pp. 40–42.

56. Ibid., p. 42.

57. See Jon Pareles, "Street Smarts Beyond Rap's Braggadocio," *New York Times* (July 23, 1989), Arts and Leisure section, p. H25.

58. Lyn Francis, "Chess Talk in Washington Square Park: Control in a Miniature World" (Paper for Aesthetics of Everyday Life, course taught in the Department of Performance Studies, New York University, Spring 1986).

59. Franco Moretti, *Signs Taken for Wonders: Essays in the Sociology of Literary Forms* (London: Verso, 1983), p. 116.

60. Michel de Certeau, "Practices of Space," *On Signs,* ed. Marshall Blonsky (Baltimore: Johns Hopkins University Press, 1985), p. 129. See also Michel De Certeau, *The Practice of Everyday Life,* trans. Steven F. Rendall (Berkeley: University of California Press, 1984).

NOTES

SELECTED BIBLIOGRAPHY

Abrahams, Roger D. *Jump-Rope Rhymes: A Dictionary.* Austin: University of Texas Press, 1980.

————, and L. Rankin. *Counting-out Rhymes: A Dictionary.* Austin: University of Texas Press, 1980.

Ariès, Philippe. *Centuries of Childhood.* New York: Knopf, 1962.

Avedon, E. M. and Brian Sutton-Smith, eds. *The Study of Games.* New York: John Wiley, 1971.

Bronner, Simon J. *American Children's Folklore.* Little Rock, Ark.: August House, 1988.

Callois, Roger. *Man, Play, and Games.* New York: The Free Press, 1961.

Cavallo, Dominick. *Muscles and Morals: Organized Playgrounds and Urban Reform, 1880–1920.* Philadelphia: University of Pennsylvania Press, 1981.

Csiszentmihalyi, Mihaly. *Flow Studies of Enjoyment.* PHS Grant Report, University of Chicago, 1974.

Culin, Stewart. "Street Games of Boys in Brooklyn." *Journal of American Folklore* 4 (1891): 221–237.

Douglas, Norman. *London Street Games.* 1916. Reprint, London: Chatto and Windus, 1931, New York: Johnson Reprint Corporation, 1969.

Ferretti, Fred. *The Great American Book of Sidewalk, Stoop, Dirt, Curb, and Alley.* New York: Workman Publishing Co., 1975.

Fine, Gary Alan. "Children and Their Culture: Exploring Newell's Paradox." *Western Folklore* 39, no. 3 (July 1980): 170–183.

Goffman, Erving. "Fun in Games." In *Encounters.* Indianapolis: Bobbs-Merrill, 1961.

Gomme, Alice Bertha. *The Traditional Games of England, Scotland, and Ireland.* 2 vols. 1894, 1898. Reprint, New York: Dover Publications, 1964.

Goodman, Cary. *Choosing Sides: Playground and Street Life on the Lower East Side.* New York: Schocken Books, 1979.

Hale, Ethel and Oliver. "From Sidewalk, Gutter and Stoop: Being a Chronicle of Children's Play and Game Activity." Manuscript, 2 packages, New York Public Library, 1938.

Halpert, Herbert. "Folk Rhymes of New York City Children." Master's thesis, Columbia University, 1946.

Hawes, Bess Lomax, "Law and Order on the Playground." In *Games in Education and Development,* ed. Loyda M. Shears and Eli M. Bower. Springfield, Ill.: Charles C. Thomas, 1974.

————, and Bessie Jones. *Step It Down: Games, Plays, Songs, and Stories from the Afro-American Heritage.* New York: Harper & Row, 1972.

Herland, George. *Centuries of Childhood in New York: A Celebration on the Occasion of the 275th Anniversary of Trinity School.* New York: The New-York Historical Society and Trinity School, 1984.

Horne, Philip Field. "Outdoor Recreation in Colonial New York." Master's thesis, State University of New York College, 1976.

Huizinga, Johan. *Homo Ludens: A Study of the Play Element in Culture.* London: Routledge and Kegan Paul, 1949; reprint, Boston: Beacon Press, 1955.

Kirshenblatt-Gimblett, Barbara. "The Future of Folklore Studies in America: The Urban Frontier." *Folklore Forum* 16 (Fall 1983): 175–233.

Knapp, Mary and Herbert. *One Potato, Two Potato . . .: The Secret Education of American Children.* New York: W. W. Norton and Co., 1976.

Mathias, Elizabeth. "From Folklore to Mass Culture: Dynamics of Acculturation in the Games of Italian Men." Ph.D. dissertation, University of Pennsylvania, 1974.

Mergen, Bernard. *Play and Playthings: A Reference Guide.* Westport, Conn.: Greenwood Press, 1982.

Milberg, Alan. *Street Games.* New York: McGraw-Hill, 1976.

Miska, Maxine, and I. Sheldon Posen. *Tradition and Community in the Urban Neighborhood: Making Brooklyn Home.* New York: Brooklyn Education and Cultural Alliance, 1983.

Nasaw, David. *Children of the City: At Work and at Play, 1900–1920.* New York: Doubleday, 1985.

Newell, William Wells. *Games and Songs of American Children.* New York: Harper and Brothers, 1883. Reprint, New York: Dover Publications, 1963.

Opie, Iona and Peter. *Children's Games in Street and Playground.* Oxford: Clarendon Press, 1969.

————. *The Lore and Language of Schoolchildren.* London: Oxford University Press, 1959.

Riis, Jacob. *Children of the Poor.* New York: Charles Scribner's Sons, 1892.

Rosenzweig, Roy. "Middle Class Parks and Working Class Play: The Struggle over Recreational Space in Worchester, Massachusetts, 1870–1910." *Radical History Review* 21 (Winter 1979–80): 31–46.

Schermerhorn, Gene. *Letters to Phil: Memories of a New York Boyhood, 1848–1856.* Foreword by Brendan Gill. (New York: New York Bound Books, 1982).

Schwartz, Jane. *Caught.* New York: Available Press/Ballantine Books, 1985.

Smith, Robert Paul. *"Where Did You Go?" "Out." "What Did You Do?" "Nothing."* New York: W. W. Norton and Co., 1957.

Sutton-Smith, Brian. *The Folkgames of Children.* Austin: University of Texas Press, 1972.

————. *A History of Children's Play: The New Zealand Playground, 1840–1950.* Philadelphia: University of Pennsylvania Press, 1981.

Tuan, Yi-Fu. *Space and Place: The Perspective of Experience.* Minneapolis: University of Minnesota Press, 1977.

von Hartz, John. *New York Street Kids.* New York: Dover Publications, 1978.

Ward, Colin. *A Child in the City.* New York: Pantheon Books, 1978.

Winkleman, Michael. *The Fragility of Turf: The Neighborhoods of New York City.* Albany: New York State Education Department, New York State Museum, Division of Research and Collections, 1986.

Zerner, Charles J. "The Street Hearth of Play: Children in the City." *Landscape* 22 (Autumn 1977): 19–30.

INDEX